AF435071

THE LOUISVILLE REVIEW

WINTER/SPRING 2024

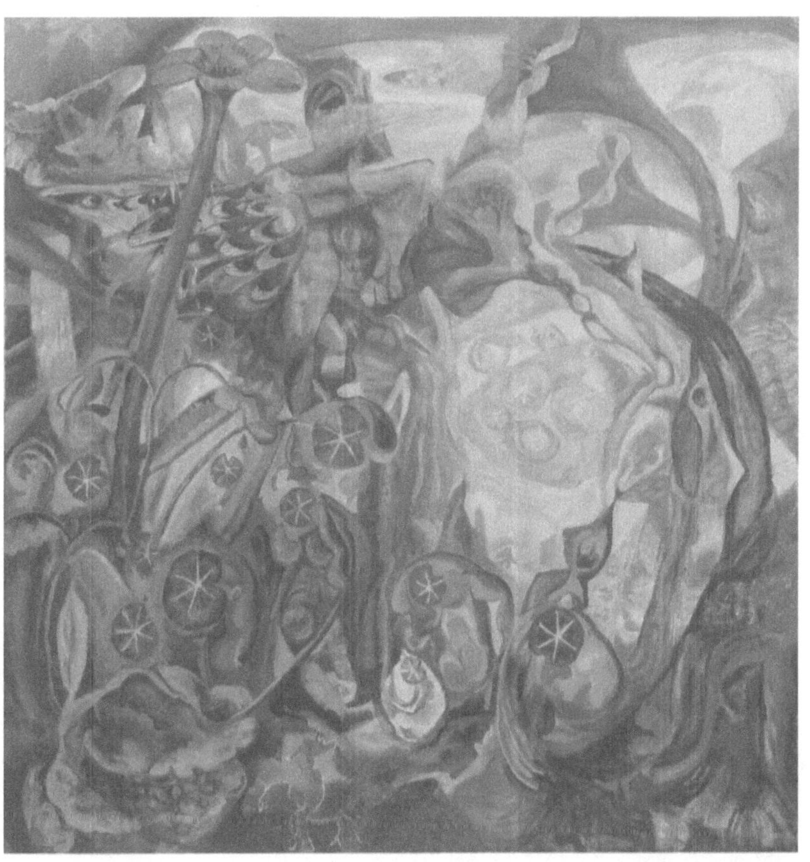

Laurie Fader, *Trumpets*

94

The Louisville Review

Editor	Sena Jeter Naslund
Associate Editor	Flora K. Schildknecht
Managing Editor	Amy Foos Kapoor
Guest Poetry Editor	Jonathan Weinert*
Guest Fiction Editor	Mary Popham*
Cornerstone Editor	Betsy Woods
Technical Director	Ron Schildknecht
Financial Director	John Morgan

* Poetry and fiction selections are also made by Editor Sena Jeter Naslund
  and Associate Editor Flora K. Schildknecht.

TLR publishes two volumes each year. Visit our website for complete guidelines,
back issues, subscriptions, and more: www.louisvillereview.org.

Like us on Facebook: www.facebook.com/TheLouisvilleReview
Follow us on Twitter @TheLouRev

Questions? Please note our email and mailing addresses:

managingeditor@louisvillereview.org

The Louisville Review Corp.
1436 St. James Court #1
Louisville, Kentucky 40208

This issue: $10 ppd
Sample copy: $5 ppd
Subscriptions: One year, $18; two years, $36; three years, $54 plus $2 shipping
Subscribers outside the United States please add $35/year for shipping.

Text and cover printed in the United States.
Cover and interior design by Jonathan Weinert.

Cover artwork: Laurie Fader, *Trumpets*. Oil on canvas, 52" x 50." Photographed by
Ron Schildknecht.

The Louisville Review is a not-for-profit publication.
The Louisville Review Corporation is a member of the Community of Literary
Magazines and Presses.

The Louisville Review's

NATIONAL POETRY BOOK CONTEST

is now open!

TLR's **National Poetry Book Contest,** a first-book poetry contest
open to poets in the United States, is accepting submissions
June 1–August 31, 2024.

The contest invites poets who have not yet published a book of poetry
to send manuscripts of 65 pages and under for review.

The entry fee of $35 includes a 1-year print subscription to
The Louisville Review. Winner will receive print publication
of their book through *The Louisville Review's* Fleur-de-Lis Press
in 2025, 25 author copies, and distribution through Barnes & Noble
and Amazon. Finalists will receive publication of a selected, previously
unpublished poem in *The Louisville Review.*

For details, visit Submittable.com at https://thelouisvillereviewfleur-
de-lispress.submittable.com/submit/297313/the-louisville-reviews-
national-poetry-book-contest

Direct questions to managingeditor@louisvillereview.org

Our **first contest as an independent journal** is made possible by a
generous grant from the Snowy Owl Foundation.

Associate Editor's Note

For the cover of this issue of *The Louisville Review* we are delighted to feature **Laurie Fader**'s painting, *Trumpets*. At once formally complex and fantastical, the painting is accompanied by Fader's "Cover Artist's Statement: Trumpets" that narrates the creation of the painting—as well as the biological precarity and the gamut of stylistic influences that inform the work.

A poem from **Emily Jane O'Dell**, "Night of Shooting Stars," in English and translated to the Burmese with co-translator **Ein Kyi Phyu**, opens this issue. O'Dell's poem engages the horrific civil war that continues to unfold in Myanmar, but also associatively recalls the many deadly wars playing out in the world today, asserting the value of the literary arts for bearing witness to these tragic conflicts.

In this issue we're also proud to include poetry from not one *but two* soon-to-be-published collections, by **Kathleen Driskell** from *Goat-Footed Gods*, forthcoming from Carnegie-Mellon University Press, and by **Julie Marie Wade** from *Quick Change Artist*, selected by Octavio Quintanilla for the Anhinga Press Poetry Prize.

I'm tickled that a healthy portion of the prose in *TLR* 94 has something of the imprint of childhood and adolescence, from the excitement and danger of **Bethany Bruno**'s "Fed to the Gators," to "Out Too Deep" by **Pamela Baker**, that addresses the mysteries of the need for belonging in childhood. Likewise, new nonfiction by Australian author **Rebekah Clarkson**, "Dominion," investigates the ambiguities of youthful desire for, and aversion to, commitments to animals, people, and religion. Short fiction by **Wen-Shing Ho**, "Wild Ginger Flower on the Rock," celebrates intergenerational bonds and transports readers into family life in post-pandemic China.

Over the years *The Louisville Review* has held several poetry book contests, the last in 2002, judged by Maura Stanton. With this issue we are proud to open submissions from July 1 through August 31 for our first **National Poetry Book Contest** as an independent journal. Thanks to essential support from the **Snowy Owl Foundation**, the contest will provide publication of a first book of poetry from *The Louisville Review*'s Fleur-de-Lis Press.

The work we do at *TLR* would not be possible without the vital contributions of our guest editors for each issue, and I extend our heartfelt thanks to our guest poetry editor, who, along with myself, selected the poetry for this issue of *TLR*:

Jonathan Weinert is a 2005 graduate of Spalding's Naslund-Mann Graduate School of Writing. He is the author of the poetry collections *A Slow Green Sleep*, winner of the Saturnalia Books Editors Prize, *In the Mode of Disappearance*, winner of the Nightboat Poetry Prize, and *Thirteen Small Apostrophes*, a chapbook. He is co-editor of *Until Everything Is Continuous Again: American Poets on the Recent Work of W. S. Merwin*, and is a contributor to *Traces: Sand and Snow in Symbiosis*, an anthology of ekphrastic poems by Anglophone and Arabophone poets, recently released by Middle Creek Publishing.

Likewise, I must extend our deep gratitude to our guest fiction editor, who along with Editor **Sena Jeter Naslund** selected the fiction for this issue:

Mary Popham is a 2003 graduate of Spalding's Naslund-Mann Graduate School of Writing. Her novels set in Central Kentucky in the early 1900s are *Back Home in Landing Run*, *The Wife Takes a Farmer*, and *Emmalene of Landing Run*, with a forthcoming title, *Angel of Landing Run*. She leads a writing group, the Cherokee Roundtable; and presents a program, "Writing Your Life Story."

Many thanks to **Betsy Woods** for her continued service as Editor of Cornerstone, *The Louisville Review*'s section of poetry by young writers in grades K–12.

Finally, a huge and sincere thank you to our Managing Editor, **Amy Foos Kapoor**, who has graciously donated her time to help bring this issue into being.

—Flora K. Schildknecht, Associate Editor

Table of Contents

Poetry

Nonfiction

Fiction

Cornerstone

Poetry

Emily Jane O'Dell

Night of Shooting Stars

Tonight, it's raining
bombs like shooting stars.

Prisoners of twilight,
we're dreaming of dawn.

Hear
the death rattle
of the phantom
haunting this land?

Hear
the cry of the
morning
waiting to be born?

Though the earth is scorched,
my flip-flops are lined
with velvet.

Spellbound by the moon,
I tread gently on the ashes
of my home.

Is it the morning dew
or just tears
hydrating my
sunken cheeks?

ကြယ်ကြွေည

ဒီည မိုးက ရွာနေ
ဖုံးတွေ ကြယ်တွေလို့ ကြွေကျ

ဆည်းဆာရဲ့ အကျဉ်းသား
ရောင်နီကို မက်တဲ့ တို့ရဲ့ အိပ်မက်များ

တခြောက်ခြောက် အသံတွေကြား
ဒီမြေကို စိုးမိုးတဲ့ တစ္ဆေရဲ့
မရဏဆင့်ခေါ်သံကို ကြား

မင်းကြားလား
မွေးဖွားဖို့ ငင့်လင့်နေတဲ့
မနက်ခင်းရဲ့ ဟစ်ကြွေးသံကို မင်းကြားလား

ပထဝီမြေကြီး ငရဲမီးလို့ တောက်လောင်နေလဲ
ရှေ့ခရီးလမ်းကို ကတ္တီပါဖိနပ်နဲ့ လျှောက်လှုမ်းနေဆဲ

လကို တမ်းတမိတဲ့ ကျွန်မရဲ့ မျက်လုံးများ
မီးသင့်အိမ်တွေရဲ့ ပြာတွေပေါ်မှာ ညင်သာစွာ လမ်းလျှောက်သွား

အိုး... ပါးပြင်ပေါ်မှာ
နှင်းရည်တွေလား
မျက်ရည်လား

Closing my eyes,
I see a transboy
in Mandalay
I have
yet to meet.

The sun
rising in my heart
is about
to shine
on my home.

မျက်လွှာကို ရှုရှုမ့ိတ်လိုက်တာ
အပြင်မှာ မတွေ့လိုက်ရသေးတဲ့
မန္တလေးက ယောက်ျားလျာကို မြင်ယောင်လာ

နှလုံးသားထဲက
ရဲတက်လာတဲ့ နေဝန်း
တို့အိမ်တွေပေါ်မှာ
ရောင်ခြည်ဖြာတော့မည် မကြာ။

translated to the Burmese by co-translators Emily Jane O'Dell and Ein Kyi Phyu.

Miles Waggener

Algorithmic Companion

If not quite mind then   then a yellow logo's not-gray
     gas station light & empty auditorium
sky over dead ember heartland   & if not you/them
     then how have I found myself so far away

from all I've known?   Nostalgia's phantoms fray
     into split optics.   Blood's high tension wires thrum
through fields in my chest.   My phone's aquarium
     glow flickers to a newly-made-for-me display:

if not me, then   my mother on her knees,
     her hands folded across her childhood bed
praying to a god   only her mother believes in.

     She's asking a windy shape   in the mind's wind
back then in her time   or in mine   for peace.
     We watch her & know the war will never end.

Gaylord Brewer

Whit Monday

I passed the last scattered
houses of the last village,
the final human voices, passed
beneath a canopy of birch,
its encryptions of shadow,
out into a wide and empty sky.
I passed the boarded farmhouse,
crossed vast fields
of wheat and feed corn,
vineyards, sunflower without bloom.
I kept walking, followed
the tireless urging of the road,
verges of thistle and chaos,
continued neither trusting nor faithless
until hat and shirt were dark stains,
my bag weighed of stone,
until the pavement ended,
and kept on, walking a cracked
earth, glad for my searing thirst,
until day passed overhead,
until all birdsong silenced.
No hush of wind, laughing waterfall,
until feet were numb and torn,
until no god would have me,
and walked on, my back to the sun,
ascended into the burning
hills and even then farther on.
But it was no good.
I will tell you that I could not
outwalk the years never to return,
outwalk the lost names of everything,
could not escape myself.

Alexander Etheridge

Guiding Fire

after Rolf Jacobsen

As a way to get back home
I look everywhere for the roads
I barely recall—In the absolute

quiet, you can hear
other voices
guiding you back
again—In the deep end of November

dusks, you begin to see

paper lanterns light up
along the old dirt roads—
It takes so long to get there

and it takes another lifetime
walking slowly

toward home.

Dianne Aprile

Where We Were Going

I grew up on a suburban road
named for a farmer's field—Brownlee.
A lee is another word for meadow,
my mother told me. *You'll find it*
often in crossword puzzles.

She was right about that. Even now
when I see the word —each letter
filling an empty block, sign of
something larger than itself—
I think of her and how

she moved from town
to that newly graveled lane
at a tender 29, a month before
she birthed me, her first daughter,
though she couldn't have known
I'd be her only one, not then—
nor could she have guessed
I'd be that age myself

when she died. I tried to solve it,
Is 29 the *X* of our equation—
the crosswalk where her life
and mine intersected
and then did not.

Dianne Aprile

Dark Circles

Unwillingly
I have always worn them
half-circles really,
half moons turned inside out,
not lunar pale but
dusk and shadow, squatting
dim beneath my eyes
into corners hard to reach.
Hard to hide.

I have worn them,
as well, beneath my skin
but more a spiral than a circle,
a deeper dark
than flesh could bear.
A black curl
beneath my hide
coiled out of sight
looped to my mind.

Years back, at some expense
I dabbed that dark with balm;
camouflage and cover up
obscured a smoke-tinged tone.
But now I'm keen to lift
the shade, let it bloom.
the gloom, the murk,
the mark of me: Blood coursing
close to the surface,
refusing to be
calm.

Derek Mong

Twilight in Late May

In that hour

     after raking peat moss through raised beds—

     after the heat tips back   behind the treetops

          like a child surprised by a rocker—

after a bath and a beer and stew

     that stretches a belt loop—

in that hour

when you & your mother   flip through *New Yorker* cartoons

     and sip   soda from bottles bursting with sun—

   in that hour when I sway

     shirtless under the ceiling fan—I'm a candle flame,

     a weathervane—

in that hour   when the hour distills   to sweat

on your temple—   you swipe it dry.   Sometimes it's that simple.

❧

All day we churned the dirt.

I dipped a trowel four inches down and found a pair of grubs.

You tossed one in the patch of yard the starling guard.

We turned then to starts—tomatoes, cukes—still harbored in egg
    carton cups

which would, when gently shook, produce

a white circuitry of roots.

I held one up—its first and final taste of air—then let it brush

your wrists and palm.

You tucked it in—*snug*, you said, *in the ditch we dug.*

❧

As we danced   in the foyer

before dinner   your shadow   slipped free from your heel

                to float   like a bubble

in a spirit level—   and R.E.M. (your   favorite) filled the radio—

                            and our faces   warmed slowly

like an exposure   after the aperture   closes.

A contrail fades across our swathe of sky.

Tonight, your parents stay up late to talk; the stalks beneath their
          windows rise.

Derek Mong

To a Study Desk on the Second Floor of the William Howard Doane Library

Blonde box hopscotched
with graffiti
windowless vessel
I'd melt into

before a fluorescent
reflection blinks
out across this sea
of green tile

once there was nothing
I couldn't conjure
in your diorama
words theories dreams

a firefly's cursive
beam or that rolodex
of garrulous drafts
who do you now

Cousteau
in your diving bell
or are you always
this empty as new frost

Rob MacDonald

Piano

                                    I do not look forward

           to hearing, again,

                           the first eight notes

    when asked about fear

                    of "Hallelujah"

       of death

               emanating from the piano downstairs.

     the author said that

                 As the widow cycles through those notes

the characters in her novels are unaware that

                    her husband's final days

      the last pages

          are approaching

                 feel nothing

        echo

            when the book

     with reluctance.

                is closed

        and set gently

   Down—I hear it now

                 on the bedside table

       through the floorboards.

I do not look forward.

Rob MacDonald

Korobeiniki

        Schuyler says
   he can see
          The young peddler
             Among Us everywhere—
trash can, big toe, the Champion
          knew the cost of a
   logo. I understand.
      night
            Somewhere, I'm still
         with Katya:
stacking the seven Tetris blocks—
              one turquoise ring.
        O, T, Z, S, J, L,
  He left to prove his worth and
        I—
           might have earned her as a wife
     if not for
       the melody accelerating faster than
   the invisible hand,
      an armed man,
           hypnotized by the song
   the nightmare.
       of the coins
   in the peddler's pocket
            "Make it stop,"
      Schuyler says.

Rob MacDonald

Static

Today reminds me of
Forgetting is not
yesterday
in that it's making
fun. Of
me
want to punch a hole in this
course, remembering is a
station wagon.
"What's a station wagon?"
my Gen Z co-workers ask.
"It's a
burden, the
bland sort of brick
occupying space
in an otherwise compelling
16-year-old's
universe. It's a
whole summer spent loading
and unloading the same
vehicle for delivering
roller coaster.
disappointment.
It's what
today reminds me of."

Ace Boggess

An Announcement

I have nothing to say.
I thought I knew what I meant when I muttered
first words of a gray morning;
couldn't comprehend emptiness
that came when I spoke, blank lines I wrote.
My pen has run out of ink.

I have nothing to say,
yet go on saying it anyway
like a man next to you on the bus
who doesn't realize engine whirs &
thub thub thub of the tires
add more depth of meaning to your life.

I have nothing to say—
a rattletrap clamor, a B-flat in the pipes.
My speech is the singsong sweetness
of an ice-cream truck on another street.
Too late, too late! You've heard my nonsense,
jabberwocky, innuendo without invitation,

benediction of burbles, sandpaper scraping a nail.
Try to remember the whispers,
not clogged discombobulations of my monologue
as you leave here with less than you started,
your head abuzz, ablur, oblique
from all the nothingness I've shared.

Kathleen Driskell

Promise

The gods say *c'mon*,
we're offering you life
everlasting, but I'd rather
have hubris, rancor,

a greasy pork chop,
regular old smut,
a jug full of green
wine instead of
a very good glass

of claret with its nose
full of cherry and black
dirt. Sure. I know
what's good for me,

but I don't want it.
They shrug, say okay,
feels, though, like we ought to
give you some-

thing. They glance around.
Well, there's this,
they say, it's not much
to look at but here
go ahead and take it
anyway, take this bruised
old boot, mortality.

Kathleen Driskell

Blake Looking Through Trees

I regret that I did not take you out
into the backyard in late spring,
in mid-morning, a tattered old tree
of paradise quilt folded under my arm,
until I unfurled it, allowing it to waft
to the grass, settling like a lumpy square,
and that we didn't lay there until the sun
broke through a Green Hawthorne's leafy
crown, filling it with flickering light.
I would have told you then about Blake
and how as a child he hiked beyond
the busy London streets, slimy and
fouled by horses and drunks, how
he lay recumbent, alone for hours,
under glorious trees like these, imagining
that the winking lights were angels,
his angels, come to reveal themselves.
Knowing myself, I might have said
to you I do not believe in angels, nor
God—nor anything else supernatural.
But I hope I would have urged you
to see whatever you might see, my
darlings, to believe whatever you
might need or even want to believe.

Charles O. Hartman

Sweet Almond

Lest the great shout that is spring
happen wholly without us
this unhappy year, we walk

out under buds and birdsongs,
sometimes in the same high tree,
and we look up earnestly

the names of both, to name them
to each other, if only
over the phone, or leave them

at each other's distant door:
a vase of names, a quiet
bouquet of would-be touches.

It troubles, some, to fathom how
lucky we are that words come
(maybe with a thumb-sized glimpse

on a thumb-smudged screen)
so close to satisfying
the needs that make us creatures.

Enough of this human stuff—
this closet, window chatter.
The tree that accosted me

today, with its five-fold pale
petals in tens of thousands
and serrated leaves, gave me

a message to pass along.
As near as I can recall,
this was it. Oh, and this too:

come out, all the way out,
not out of words—bring the words—
but into the shouts of birds.

Charles O. Hartman

You Too, Bro?

Whatever the crow
recovers, it isn't
dignity. Mobbed, jayed,

she flaps to a backup branch
& resettles feathers.
If she's still there,

pal, it's not to brood
—nowhere in view, really,
to move to, wide as her prospect

is. No point
regurgitating old quarrels
in a world picked clean.

Who killed whom
i' th' Capitol? Does it matter
at this remove?

The sun is fire
& gives fire
everything. This glittering world

will kill us all.
If I'm still here
I'm gathering

what light I can. If not,
I did. (& what jays,
mate, drive you?)

Charles O. Hartman

Remembered Scars

On one thigh the white arc—
where a wire fence,
climbed in eighth grade

to retrieve a soccer ball, exacted
penalty not deep but visibly
stubborn—stood out

against the pallor
for two decades
or three: when did I last

see it and apologize
to the leg or for the leg
as its custodian?

And then where my knife
whittling the image
of a boat slipped

and turned up a flap of flesh
just above the other knee,
the knee declared

in sun and pool and bed
for more years than I can recall
the knife, the slip.

How many years
can be recalled, scored
as they are? In skin,

collagen fibers
strew. A scar is where,
repairing, they align. A time ago

I saw the marks. Behold
me, immaculate, bereft,
outliving them.

Teresa Cader

When Syrinx Turns Into a Lilac Bush

On the hill of lilacs at the Arboretum, blue blossoms peak
    on hardy stems, as if Syrinx, safe from Pan, reveled

in noonday sun, and Whitman, tired of mourning,
    clipped a branch, not for a coffin but the vase on his desk.

I planted three lilac trees in the rock garden my father built,
    the blue my favorite, lasting long after the others died,

a miracle of sorts, since I was a negligent gardener,
    harming the trees I loved but didn't know how to save.

Some say Pan chased Syrinx because he loved her beauty;
    others say he tried to rape her; maybe it was both.

My daughter and I vacationed at the Wentworth Hotel,
    named for the Tory governor who left behind a lilac garden,

the first in America, copied by Washington and Jefferson,
    the Persian *lilak* seeding itself into American history.

At fifteen I found *Leaves of Grass* in my father's bookcase:
    Whitman's narcissistic self-love, obsessive sex, shocked me.

Chosen to seek foreign and unweathered shores, I wrote about
    myself that night in my first poem. Many years later I'd find

in my father's mountain village the family he'd never named,
    survivors of the Hapsburgs, Hitler, then Stalin,

and two centuries hell-bent on erasing their language—
	upended by immigration to America—*our wretched refuse.*

My daughters have become what I call *full* Americans, free
	from the weight of otherness and migration stories,

my father's and grandparents' papers pressed under books
	in trunks, irrelevant, unless found by a curious child.

Teresa Cader

Lines by Wisława Szymborska Rearranged as Elegy

All imperfection is easier to tolerate in small doses.
I'm working on the world, revised, improved edition.
Those crafty hedgehogs drafting aphorisms after dark.

The exam is History of Mankind.
Two monkeys, chained to the floor, sit on the windowsill.
Don't ask, I can't say, I don't know.

To tell right from wrong, "ours" from "theirs."
You'll see how we give birth among the ruins.
A rose? A rose? What could that be?

The most pressing questions are naive ones.
All the cameras have gone to another war.
History rounds off skeletons to zero.

Forgive me, distant wars, for bringing flowers home.
In my dreams I paint like Vermeer van Delft.
A little poem, a sigh, at the cost of indescribable losses.

translations of Wisława Szymborska by Stanislaw Barańczak and Clare Cavanagh

Elizabeth Majerus

The Six Dreaming Languages

Orthos

For the speaking of intuitive truths; for the recitation of obscure grievances; for the revisiting of oaths and pledges previously recited without comprehension.

Tumulese

The tongue that carries awkward, unbalanced loads. The tongue that shows you what a thing is not and insistently reveals that it *is* that thing.

Min

For food talk, speeches employed in rituals of courtship, and tales told along the road on journeys.

Ubbuh

For speaking with loved ones who have the faces, bodies, smells, or ineffable auras of other unrelated persons; for speaking with loved ones no longer present in the world of waking who visit the realm of sleep.

Slip Tongue

The highest play of wordsmiths from every corner of the realm; the tongue of terrifying jokes and deep, confounding anecdotes.

Swarmish

Flee when you hear speech uttered in this tongue. Fly if you can.

Kevin McLellan

Ways & Means

A
Trees he looked to for faith. A chorus
above the trees. The wooden table

wasn't his. The boy walked to father

& away. The internal dialogue, *Always
you yell inside me,* circles and stings.

B
The son requests that he be
referred to as boy instead. The boy

wants to believe in visionary

practices. But the bees arbitrarily
above the buzzing geranium.

C
The boy wanted to sit at the kitchen table.
Does that make him a chair?

Once holding grain during martial law

the burlap the painter Burri reconstructed
for a piece. Does this make him a sculptor?

D
Some created from nothingness
& fell in love—

a shared "onceness" could kill

or save as could fiction & the new
meanings of "overflow." & "tranquility."

E
The son became man
having learned: desire,

arbitrariness & narration

but the acceptance hole
remains in burlap.

F
Another dream provided the son
another new lover. The son wakes

& tries to remember their faces

kissing. *Freely espousing?* a narrator
asked? He exclaimed, *Impossible!*

G
The son's been observing a mason
ever since hearing him, *An objective position's*

fine under most circumstances, but not when

it comes to death. The son daydreams of him,
wants to see him epoxy & cement.

H
The son begins to write his memoir, *The new*
potato's skin—punctured by a spade

at first frost—smells of father. He fears & longs for

the words "supreme" & "sacred" as convincingly
as Graham & Stevens writes them.

I
The son watched Comăneci in Montreal
receive a perfect 10 & he differently eyed

the men close. Back at school in rural America

the gym teacher said, *Boys don't do gymnastics*
after he said, *I want to learn gymnastics.*

J
Visualization—the son stares
out windows, first looking

at trees & then the portal

between one & his internal one—
sees particulates & feels he's near.

K
Espousal.
Espouse.

Exposed.

Expository.
Expound.

L
Imagine the inflamed throat of a narrator
giving birth to the word

"hitherto" says the son. Is this said

to shed light on the separating &
unite the inside from out?

M
As Dragulescu waits for the average
of two flights—the almost-

perfect signature vault—another

gymnast's taken away on a stretcher.
Or is it a gurney?

N
What is the point if we're not living for
one another? A documentarian

captures rituals & adds metaphors.

For example: two wild birds fly
above a road that becomes the horizon.

O
The son migrated… no, moved… no,
ran away… far away at first & he has

borders… no actual fences or guards.

He created them in the abstract
to limit his movement. Is this art?

P
The effect of Burri's openings
could be described as

melting or fraying, though some

have the appearance of bullet
holes or human ones.

Q
He who sculpted said, *I must
function as surface,*

material & idea, which is why

openings are necessary. Ask
any woodpecker.

R

As fast as the blinking
eye or flickering tongue

& the ants will continue

to soldier on without saying
"Hooah!" or "Booyah!"

S

Naturally, herons migrate, but earlier this year
& without notice. The once-rock now

not unlike water, is a sensory mirror

for those who choose to touch it. Or
it's vitrified & sometimes it even holds itself.

T

The geranium was left outside. The son
brought in frostbite. He found no comfort

sitting by triple-paned windows & their

underwater sounding, but comfort
with scratchy cartwheeling leaves.

U

A favorite to win-it-all
on the high bar Malone

didn't fall to the mat

below like he did
during qualifications.

V
Andrianov.
Fedorchenko.

Hoffman.

Tsukahara.
Watanabe.

W
He is a non-believer, but believes
he's finally accepted his father's

need for unrest. The desk-lamp

on the kitchen table lit itself
late last night. He hadn't turned it on.

X
Though forgotten
home is abstract—

the geranium will go

back to bed
like clockwork anyway.

Y
There's an innate order to things.
But who or what decides? Woodpeckers.

Ants. The chorus above the trees

& the trees. Holes? Maybe they know?
There's an intimate order to things.

Z
The father learned to assault
the kitchen table & the son

learned to eat the food

from his table which is why
the chorus still waits for rest.

John Surowiecki

[Some Time during Every Lovely Day a]

Some time during every lovely day a
biplane makes its way across the sky
stuttering and stalling like an old
and iffy heart. Often it returns for a closer look,
making sure that when Kowarsky
says O what a lovely day it is
he knows exactly what he's talking
about since lovely days are
fewer and fewer in life. It's
your basic death-math. The closer
you get to your end, the more there is
to appreciate and the less there
actually is. For a few more sunsets
goldfinches will burst into flames
like sheets of flash paper and for a few
more summer afternoons
the smell of raspberries
will supersaturate the world.

John Surowiecki

[Kowarsky at the DMV]

He can be the woman with the triad of moles
below her left ear, just like the sky-
hunter's belt of pelts dot dot dot.
He can be the boy-
faced man, the man-faced girl, the baby-
faced grandfather, the dog-faced babe, the cat-
faced *ingénue*.
At the other end of the room,
where people are being photographed,
he can be the brown-stained man stealing heat
or the professorial young man whose head
rests on the nest of a blue Italian scarf:
except he, Kowarsky,
has never been street-smart
or book-smart or SAT-smart.
He's kitchen-table-smart,
learning little things,
searching for insignificances
and loopholes and easy way outs
and all the while wondering if
his number will ever come up.

Susan Campbell Bartoletti

I Would I Would

sit in my window and let down
my hair and help you climb in
if only you loved me I would
bite a poisoned apple prick
my finger and sleep one
hundred years I could waiting
for your kiss I would walk
with bleeding feet I could
spin straw into gold give up
my voice my first born I would
wrap myself around a limb
and please you with forbidden
fruit I would make you love me
good I could spend six months
in Hades missing sunlight
the turn of leaves in fall and snow
I would believe me I could
if only you loved me

Kevin Grauke

Bricklayers

Down the street, four workers are bricking
the bland fronts of three new row houses.
From my porch, I watch them while I work
on broken poems, including one about them.

The space they're filling used to be empty—
the abandoned lot of a long-dead business,
home to nothing but rocks and yellow weeds,
but now here they are, sweating out their labor.

Their sure hands guide trowels to the rhythm
of a radio's reggae while I sit cool in the shade,
fiddling with words—sounds, for God's sake—
fretting over syllables and the weights of stress.

Not once do they squint against the sun to look
my way. But can you blame them? After all,
what am I? Just a builder of clouds, puffs of air.
And them? Makers of things meant to serve, last.

Though perhaps not forever, what with the world
going as it is. So which will persist longer, black
marks on paper or the heft of mortared bricks?
Neither, maybe, in truth, here along the wet coast.

Contempt tends to teach punishing lessons.
Their bricks, my poems: the same in the end.
Both will crumble in the face of what may show
itself this Thursday or next or the next. Because time

has come today, just as the Chambers Brothers
said it would back in sixty-seven, in ten minutes
of the most innocent psychedelic soul—back
when the future was still free love and paisley.

Yes, time has come today. So, builders, let's build
everything high and wide. Let's build like the spark
might never die, like there's no no tomorrow—
you your fired-clay elegies, me my iambic crypts.

Dan Pinkerton

Saint Teresa of Avila

Yesterday in the Wendy's drive-thru I argued that every piece of art is
    an affront to death since
art provides a stay against time. Time is in cahoots with death, leading
    us all
by the bridle toward the everlasting glue factory, while art preserves the
    musculature
of the horse forever. The girl behind the speaker box asked if I wanted
    fries with that.

Each poem, I went on, was the merest splinter in death's pinkie finger.
    My own portrait in the
mirror had been gummed by flaccidity and wrinkles, smudged,
    abstracted,
as though the dissatisfied artist struggled with an old eraser before
    quitting in disgust.

When I brought home the burgers in their grease-gray wrappings, my
    wife would undoubtedly
cry because I'd remembered her birthday, she a year older, the sketch
that much more muddled, this same woman who once cried that her
    birthday had been forgotten.
The server wore the most beatific expression while making my change.

I briefly thought she was St. Teresa of Avila and Bernini had brought
    her here to the east side of
Des Moines so her beauty and youth might startle the unsuspecting
    masses.
It wasn't so farfetched. Every day, with paintbrushes and gestures of
    goodwill,
we performed our resurrections.

Alan Naslund

Vin Ordinaire

It's no wonder that Grandma Nellie
had an affinity for mountains
and mountain scenery.
She spent half of her lifetime
working as a ranch cook
in the Bears Paw Mountains
near Havre, Montana.

She carried her fascination
a little further than that,
instilling in me the urge
to draw and paint mountains
as landscape art.

Hers was a kind of Grandma Moses
style, mine reminiscent of
what I had learned of Picasso.
I saw planes and angles and triangles, cubic art.

The sides of each of
my geometric form got a different color or shade
under my hand, most usually
blues and greens except for
the orange, yellow, chartreuse,
and red of sunset, sundown.

I don't remember ever trying to
paint moonlight, so maybe that
is something left for me to explore
at this late date.

What did I paint on, canvas?
Too sophisticated for Nell
and no supplies of that kind.
We painted the surface of dinner
plates, watercolors mainly.

Once our plates were dry,
Nellie varnished over the tops
of the images to give the work
a kind of permanence.

Surely you have seen dinner
plates decorated so?
Well, not originals of the kind
Nellie inspired—boughten plates.
My mother had a collection
of those. I brought her one
from Scotland from my visit there.

But you can guess that Mom
didn't display Nellie's nor my
plates with her collectibles—
the "vin ordinaire" of the genre.

Julie Marie Wade

Something Golden

In memory of Linda Ann Wade

I do not dispute the beach is beautiful, or the brown pelicans with sun on their wings, or the palm trees curvy as parentheses. Still, I like to ride my bike in a darkened room, with pop tunes effulgently blaring. Behind my eyes, I am always riding in the same tulip field, the one Aunt Linda photographed so many years ago in Skagit Valley with her high-powered lens. There are red tulips for miles on end: a scarlet ribbon of them, a carpet unrolling to the foothills & back again. But somehow among the thousands she spotted a single yellow flower & zoomed in. The daffodil was shy as a new girl on the first day of school, hunched & blushing. Always, I think, I am riding toward that flower, watching for the one blond head bobbing on the bright red sea. Most days the class ends before I find her. Most days I remember Linda is still long dead. But every now & then I catch a glimpse of something golden—the odd stalk of wheat, the daisy's sweet, coquettish face, even the dandelion in the parking strip, resplendent with unwelcome grace. For a moment, the world turns lighter, more buoyant, though my legs still burn. Linda holds her pale finger to the shutter. I can hear it click with every revolu-tion of my feet.

Julie Marie Wade

Psalm in the Spirit of the Bold Look of Kohler

I take too many showers when I'm sad.
I write bad jokes while loitering under the spigot.

For instance,

What does seaweed say when it's in trouble?

Do you give up?

Kelp!

I'm not trying to win an Oscar, even when I cry.
I think of Janet Leigh in *Psycho*, the Hershey syrup blood.

If someone stabbed me, I'd probably bleed chocolate, too.

By the way, doesn't spigot sound like a bad word to you,
a compound fracture, two epithets combined?

They get worse the longer I'm in here:
What do you call a Golden Delicious that got drunk at a frat party?

Do you give up?

Apple-sauced!

I can't bring myself to clip my toenails, which look
so vulnerable in the steam, white & soft at last.

I have my father's feet, though I will not walk in his shoes.

The shampoo we use is Tea Tree Tingle from Trader Joe's.
I try to make a joke about it, but the punchline slips out of

my hand like a clumsy bar of oatmeal soap. See how I put
the modifier in the wrong place on purpose, like it's the bar's fault,

not mine. Oatmeal reminds me that I'm hungry.
Let's have breakfast in terry cloth, talk about our woes.

Luke Wallin

Her Hand

Lie down on the table.
Time's run out.

Bone Marrow Biopsy
incoming.

A nurse offers me her hand
which I, shocked, gratefully squeeze.

When the needle for numbing
strikes, it's worst than usual and

our hands from different bodies
find their tightenings together.

Squeeze away and
don't damn move.

Then penetration of hip bone
by a twisting core of steel.

It's a horrible thing but oh that hand.
Both of you squeeze so hard that later

your hand —not hip— will remember.
Each human has 30 trillion cells,

talking and jiving electrically.
Each knows what the others need,

while they're sleeping or pontificating.
Each knows whether the other is

maintaining a heart, or foot.
Each knows what you did last summer.

And now this strange nurse who
clearly works out melds with you

as the doctor twists that
coring device again. This nurse!

Your thirty trillion and her thirty
make sixty trillion cells sharing not just

juice but everything known,
most of it unconscious, to you two.

Ten days from now you'll get results but
the 60 trillion have them now.

Hours later you'll realize your hand's in pain.
You bless that nurse and the holy grip.

You remember how long since anyone has
done to your hand with such caring.

Michael Jackman

If This Were Any Normal Time

If this were any normal time to count
the blessings I've been given late in life,
I would so gladly in these lines recount
How greatly I esteem my son and my wife,

The little aging house, our two acres' span,
The pets we've buried in these woods,
The garden where we've turned our untrained hands
To cultivating vegetables and fruits,

Six hens, all of whom we've given names,
The dogs and cat who wander on the lawn,
The pollinators, and the birds who come
To feast in the meadow we have grown.

But these are more, and less, than normal times
Where the value of such blessings steeply climbs.

Su Costa Prevost

The Two Sisters

The first time I sang for my students
I wondered if it was like hearing a defiled secret
or seeing my ripped flesh from another mirror.

Once, after school, two sisters wanted
to remove their hijabs. Just us in the room.

Do you want to see our hair?

I was transfixed by the generous unfurling
of the long brown waves down their backs
in full bounty of what is hidden then released.

Nonfiction

Laurie Fader

Cover Artist's Statement: *Trumpets*

It started with a sweeping arc reaching up across a nearly square white canvas. The first mark, casual, is made with thin blue paint. I had a vague notion of borrowing from a recent painting called *Flowercaps*, in which an umbrella-shaped flower settles itself like a hairdryer over a man's head, hiding his identity.

The big curve, which will later be part of a continuum of rhythms and counterpoints, activates the architecture of the square space. The moving organic forms are monumental, yet intimate. Varied flower shapes are inspired by the common petunia, the invasive trumpet vine, or begonia leaves that are disc-shaped with a star-like center. No image in itself is particularly charged with meaning—but their scale and intensive collaboration combine to make an unearthly world, a theater, credible but impossible.

Rich tones of red, green, and purple anchor the foreground that is built up to play off the atmospheric warmth of the saffron and pale rose distant space. Eventually, the eye must navigate through the tangle of gemlike growth. A small misshapen red figure riding a horse stands at the bottom of the canvas in contrast to an enormous bird that struggles to ascend and break free from the dense primordial thicket.

Unlikely co-hosts of Hokusai, the Brothers Grimm, and Bambi whisper to me subliminally while I paint, to inject magic into our actual crisis of biological survival.

The seepage between the illusive creatures and their background suggests that they are temporarily bound to the earth, but will soon be free of their pesky weight, at one with the light, dispersing as a cloud of pigment dust.

Rebekah Clarkson

Dominion

Pets were something other people had. Being the Minister's family, we were often invited to these people's houses for tea. There were hippies who (unfathomably) ate vegetarian food and sat on faded velvet floor cushions to do it, there was the family who lived in an old mansion renovated from canny rubbish-dump finds, there was the opulence of the Highbury's, whose little girl Leonie owned a two-story Dolls' house with electric lighting; there was the Cat Lady and the Purple Lady, named for the color of her clothing and hair and every conceivable object in her home—cups and bowls, toilet roll holder, matching fluffy seat; there was the family so poor their home was a lopsided tin shed with no lighting at all. The Kelly's, of course. And there was the Horse Lady, but she would come later.

If any of those households we visited had pets, they were of little or no interest to us.

In our family, we always knew if our mother was disapproving or repelled, especially, if she tried to hide it. She'd lift her chin and cheekbones, do a funny thing with her mouth, open her eyes a little wider. If she was truly repressing an opinion, she'd add a tight smile. Like so many other women, she'd say things were 'interesting' when what she really meant is that she hated them. But my mother didn't work hard to conceal her discomfort with other people's pets. And I understand now that she didn't really know *how* to pat a dog. I can see her now in my mind's eye, stepping out of a dog's way, raising a hand awkwardly in the air, a brief gesture toward the animal's head, more a courtesy toward the human owner, maybe a half-hearted *'oh,'* wide eyed, eyebrows raised.

Because what *would* you say to a dog?

Dogs were unpleasant and un-hygienic. I felt *sorry* for people when they fawned and fussed over their dogs. I thought *they* were unhygienic or lacking in some way: a seriousness about the things that mattered most, which was other humans. They needed to be more like us. We were a family who cared about humans. We cared about the eternal safety of their souls.

Of how a kitten came to the unfortunate state of being owned by me—or even finding her way into our home—I have no memory. I was an emotional child and I undoubtedly begged for her.

Mitsy was black and white, named by me for her little white paws. I do recall fancies of dressing a kitten in my doll's clothes, a little cardigan, perhaps a hat. To my frustration and disappointment, Mitsy did not oblige, and I hadn't owned her long before she would hiss and arch and leap if I merely entered the room. It was frustrating not knowing how to make her love me, and soon I was a little afraid of her too. Her behaviour was soon reminiscent of demon possession, which I knew about with a little authority; exorcising demons was something my father did in his job. Exorcisms were rare, but vividly enough encountered for my ten-year-old self to entertain the idea that my kitten was inflicted with the spirit of something heinous. I never said this out loud, but privately, it worried me very much.

To her feisty credit, Mitsy ran away. I arrived home from school on a grey wintry day, and she was gone. As the afternoon became early evening, I became incrementally more distressed. The whole family searched—my parents and sisters—as much perhaps to placate me as to rescue the still quite tiny kitten. I imagined her squashed under a car. As the night wore on, we all became exhausted, from my hysteria as much as anything else. We had arrived at the point of conceding: Mitsy was gone, we'd done all we could, and it was time to go to bed. I was beside myself, but no more so than when I'd finally fallen bedraggled into bed and began to hear the faintest mewing sound that I knew belonged to my badly loved kitten. Soon I was up and tossing jumpers, shoes, pulling drawers, rifling through the wardrobe. The sound was soft and intermittent but also undeniable. My parents returned to continue the search. We could all hear her; we just couldn't find her. In this frenzy of helplessness and hope, I began to entertain the idea that Mitsy had died and was communicating to me from the spirit realm—another not entirely unviable concept. Maybe she (or something else!) was taunting me from the dead.

I wanted her back, badly, but the truth was I was now completely terrified of her. This would not be the last time I felt the strange combination of longing for something whilst also being afraid of it.

As it turned out, Mitsy was huddled under the house, where it was dark and cold and smelled of packed earth and petroleum. There was a small wooden door locked with a steel bolt at the back of the house where my father stored tools and building materials and where we would sometimes crawl if we were hiding. Mitsy must have scampered in when the door was open and become trapped.

Not a kitten-haunting, then. But it was apparent I was no caretaker of cats, and Mitsy was given to the Cat Lady, the woman from our church who had a houseful of them along with two orange-haired daughters with pale feline eyes. I didn't fake putting up a fight; well out of my depth, I was relieved to be free of Mitsy's responsibility.

We visited the Cat Lady many months later and there was Mitsy, unrecognizable. Fully grown, calm, regal in her stillness—purring! This cat ignored me, and I was glad. I tried to imagine what the Cat Lady might have done to bring about Mitsy's transformation and genuinely I could not. It was both deeply relieving and mystifying. Other living beings could be changed by love; Mitsy was testament.

My best friend, Suzie Kelly, whose father was the head minister at our church, wanted a horse, and so did I, though this is not wholly true. For while I begged my father to buy me one—presenting scrapbooks, annotated textbooks and posters all devoted to my professed love of horses—I secretly hoped he wouldn't. When I pleaded for a horse, Suzie Kelly was watching in my mind's eye. Our adoration of horses was an unspoken competition.

I nearly convinced my father to buy me a retired riding-school horse called Ajax. Ajax was old and decrepit, with a slight limp and once-white coat now yellow. Though I pleaded, my heart wasn't in it. When Suzie Kelly and I discussed our first horses, we only ever conjured Black Beauty -style Stallions. My father decided against purchasing Ajax when he understood that the cost of having a dead horse removed would be more than the asking price. And while he told me he had liked the idea of an old horse because it would be slow and calm, he privately still worried I might be thrown off and sustain a head injury. He said that my mind was too important—he and I often had big theological discussions—and he couldn't bear the thought of it being damaged. I hadn't thought about the possibility of a head injury from horse riding, but then I was afraid of this too.

My fear didn't stop me going on trail-rides at the dodgy horse-riding place with Suzie Kelly and once, when we'd turned eleven, she and I went to a western horse-riding camp in our school holidays. We slept in bunk beds tucked into proper western-style wagons with wooden wheels and white covers. We had campfires and nightly devotions—it was not only mid-west, but also evangelical Christian themed.

During our week-long stay, we were each allocated a horse to look after, and could take tests in horsemanship and receive certificates and badges that testified to our abilities. How I loved tangible objects of success. I was given a Palomino pony, caramel-coloured with a pale mane and tail, named 'Princess', identical, I happily noted, to Barbie's plastic horse, which I already had on lay-by at the Bayswater Toy World. Much of my time on that camp was tending Princess in every way that could be rewarded—washing, brushing and grooming, demonstrating my ability to name the features of a western saddle (the horn and the fork, cantle and gullet)—how to hold the reins properly like two ice-cream cones and the importance of snuggling into her flank before lifting her knobbly legs to check her hooves, for what, I never learnt. Suzie Kelly was not as interested in any of this as I'd imagined. It was true her horse was not as pretty as mine, but soon I realised she was more interested in flirting with the spunky young men who ran the camp, than in getting certificates.

Under the leadership of teenagers, we had small group discussions at night in our covered wagons on the topic of what it meant to have a 'personal relationship' with Christ. As with other Christian camps I'd attended, I felt enormous pressure to respond to the 'altar call' which invariably came. I interrogated my motives and worried over whether the Holy Spirit was moving in me or whether I was merely talking to myself. I certainly wanted to be 'right with God'. The altar call came at the end of an impassioned preaching session when everyone was gathered.

We were implored to give our lives to Jesus through the public proclamation of physically standing and then proceeding to the front, where we'd be prayed over by an elder or young leader with some level of spiritual maturity. My father himself had responded to an altar call, along with thousands of others, at a Billy Graham revival when he was just fifteen years old. He had told us the story several times, and when he did, his voice would tremble, and we knew not to move until he'd finished.

I wanted the peace and the 'abundant life' promised in the Gospels, but then I wanted not to have to worry about it again. Suzie Kelly said that she planned to live large, to have lots of boyfriends and then, when she was eighteen, she would become a 'proper Christian' and settle down. How I envied her capacity to be so strategic and mercenary. At eleven years old, I would have taken inner peace over a few years of debauchery.

It was during one of the evening discussions at the Christian horse-riding camp that I heard an older girl explain that she wasn't going to 'go forward to give her life to Christ', because she'd already done that, and if she kept doing it, wouldn't God think she didn't mean it the first time? How I valued her authority on the thinking of God: that's what I wanted most—If I do this, God will think that—clarity and logic. I also craved freedom from the awful sentimentality of the altar call: the trembling and tears. Contrary to my innate childhood ability to express emotion, I was uncomfortable with the meltdowns people invariably had when they went forward, sobbing over their inherent inadequacies and new-found dependency on Jesus. I loved this dignified girl's assessment that Jesus must wish we'd just say it once, sit down, and be blessedly quiet. It pleased me enormously and when I got home, I repeated the girl's theory to my father. I repeated it word for word, as if I'd thought of it myself.

In fact, I said I *had* thought of it myself.

Had I known my father would delight in my theory with such deep gratification, such intense pleasure, that he would document and date it in his private journal, and refer to it for literally *decades* to come, I would have thought twice about sharing it, or at the very least I would have attributed it to the girl on the camp. It seems such a small thing now, a small moment, a small idea. I didn't realise how it would haunt me. I didn't know that my father would quote it back to me as one of the most wondrous moments in his parenting life. I assume it was the subtext that thrilled him most: his middle daughter had *already* given her life to Christ.

Was there anything my father wanted more in all of life than for his children—and later his grandchildren—to be bible-believing, Apostles' creed confessing Christians? His pleasure in my post-camp disclosure appeared to make him happy in a way and to a degree that I didn't properly understand, but to which I became addicted. Having my father's affirmation and endorsement was powerful, but the truth was, I had never 'gone forward;' I had not physically got out of my seat and walked to the front of a room in a public act of 'giving my life to Christ,' or had people 'lay hands on me' in prayer.

'Remember when you told me . . .' my father would begin, and I would nod, and my stomach would churn.

Not long after the camp, the following Christmas, I was given a horse bridle. My father's parents had sent an unexpected and generous cheque and I still remember the swathe of presents: white leather boot roller skates with rock-star red wheels, a feather doona, and the bridle. It didn't make sense to give me a bridle before I had a horse: how would we know if the size was correct? But I loved this bridle and took good care of it, oiling the chocolate brown leather and polishing the sturdy silver buckles and matching bit. I can still smell it. The smell of leather, for me, is the smell of hope. And hope can carry you for a surprisingly long time.

I sold the bridle a few years later to the Horse Lady. She was a no-nonsense woman in our new church in Adelaide who we carpooled with in the early years of attending our new high school. She had two horse-loving, no-nonsense daughters who wore no make-up and rolled their eyes at girls who did. She drove a red Holden station wagon and prayed for empty car parking spots at the supermarket across the road from our school.

'I need a car park, Lord,' she'd say monotone, and I'd feel my sister's thigh press against mine on the back seat and then, when she found one, the Horse Lady would manoeuvre the bulky station wagon back in and say, 'Thanks, Lord.'

We'd scuttle out of the car, smooth down our school dresses, try to lose her daughters as we crossed the road.

Fiction

Pamela Baker

Out Too Deep

Paul was around my age, maybe ten, though it's hard to tell with boys. It was the summer after fourth grade and the terror of Mrs. Finch, who can still make me squirm when I think of her. Mrs. Finch was strict and loud. She didn't allow Michael Hayes to go to the bathroom during testing, and a few minutes later Michael Hayes said, "I peed my pants."

We all stopped penciling in the bubbles to laugh and laugh until Mrs. Finch's cutting voice and dangerous face made us stop. I didn't feel good about laughing, but I couldn't help it, either. That would happen back then. I'd do something bad, like laugh or hit or gang up with others when they teased the Cunningham twins, and I was helpless to stop myself.

Michael had to scrub his chair in front of the entire class and probably failed his test. I can't think of Michael without thinking about Paul. I can't think about Paul without thinking about how little it used to take for one wrong moment, or one seemingly perfect boy, to tip my composure like a flipped canoe.

My family was one of many families renting a summer lot in a private campground on China Lake. There were several of us summer campers who ate, swam, and slept under the eastern white pines while loons haunted the lake with their wailing. Us kids, ranging from five to fifteen, roamed the campground as an unruly pack, strutting and laughing past the weekend campers with such pretention—we wanted them to know the campground was ours—while our mothers, perhaps grouchy from sleeping on a thin foam pad in a cramped communal room, yelled at us daily for tracking in the outdoors. Our mothers were always sweeping and complaining about the dirt and pine needles that clung to our wet feet, and the older kids would come to the rescue and mock our mothers saying, "What'd you expect?" because it didn't make sense: Their campers were all parked outside, in the dirt, under the pines, and alongside the rest of Maine's forested flotsam. It wasn't like they laid out carpets for us.

The safest place from the yelling was in the lake, where we all met up and planned our days according to whim and weather. Except for Saturday mornings, when all the teens slept in until noon and most of the younger kids went to town with their mothers for weekly shopping, or they went home to catch up on laundry. Saturday mornings were when all the new, weekend-getaway and week-long vacationers invaded our small beach—a cove, really, with trucked-in sand (illegal in Maine, but there were ways), two piers ending in docks, and a free-floating dock for swimmers—and basked in its newness, in being out of Massachusetts and away from their gritty, restless cities.

Most summer-long parents didn't like this glut of newcomers—outsiders, really—which is why they'd scatter back to their own nearby towns for chores. But my mother slept in later than most, and I liked the possibility of new kids who might be my age. I met Paul on one of those Saturday mornings. He was fresh to the lake and eager to make new friends. It was early, and the beach was near empty. Because our campsite had a generous view of the beach, my parents let me swim all hours, regardless of how busy or empty it was. They believed in my abilities to "swim like a fish," and I suppose in their own abilities to sense when I was in trouble should I start drowning or get approached by an iffy-looking tourist, though Maine is still a place where people believe in the relative benevolence of strangers.

Paul and I met by bobbing towards each other in the shallows. It was the kind of watery and excited hop that only children can manage without seeming strange, each of us saying "hi" in that awkward way that shows you want to be friends but don't know how to start it.

Boys could be tricky. Some never played with girls. Maybe some girls wouldn't play with boys. Name-offering was the first step in any friendship, and he offered up his name first. I showed off my underwater backflip and then he showed me his imitation of a frog. He made me laugh, and we both pretended we were frogs. Then we dared each other with underwater staring contests. We would each go under and try to sit cross-legged with our eyes open, waving to each other and making funny faces so that the other would laugh and then lose the game. I called this "a tea party" and he called it "a submarine sink."

Each of us possessed important skills. He could leap off the wharf in a perfect belly-flop, slapping the water so straight and hard that his skin turned red. But he never winced, never hinted at how it might hurt. My skill was underwater handstands. I could beat anyone. My secret was walking out to where the water was a little deeper so that balance wasn't needed—just patience and breath-holding. Both of us could hold our breath to the count of fifty.

He was a shark. I was a mermaid. He had reddish brown hair and freckles. In the water, anything was possible. Whole villages could live under the sand; there was another world buried, only open to those with gills. I wanted gills. I held my breath until my ears rung. He was taller than me. I liked his smile.

The morning was glorious. We raced each other to see who the fastest swimmer was, and I won. Paul would be part of our summer-long friend group, I'd thought, but he'd like me best. We swam out a little farther, treading water and floating on our backs—two activities I never had the patience for because it was boring. We swam to the out-deep dock where the water was way over our heads. Then we swam to the buoy line, which marked the farthest edges of where we were allowed to go. Then, strict, and loud, his mother called for him. She was a large, doughy woman who wore a bright floral swimsuit, and I had trouble matching her up to Paul, who was boney and freckled and pale. He had the kind of skin that neither burned nor tanned. It just stayed the same.

We swam back to the shallows, and I pretended not to notice his mother scolding him for going out too far. "You'll be lucky if I let you go out past your shins in this lake," she said. And, "Do I have to send you back by yourself?"

She yelled in a sharp way that made me feel small, even though I wasn't the one being yelled at. When my own mother yelled, trying to gain some semblance of order over me, I was rarely alone, rarely without the power of the pack, which I felt invincible within. There, then, on the near-empty beach, I felt stricken, like with Ms. Finch's cutting voice and dangerous face, even though I'd done nothing wrong.

"I'm sorry," Paul said, sounding defeated, weak. I felt this, too.

"Don't give me that line of bull here, mister, or you'll know what sorry is," she said. It was the heft of her that made her imposing, and the way her voice carried across the water. She wouldn't let boys, or bands of kids, or even the Pope get away with goofing around. The thought of having her for a mother scared me.

"I'm sorry," Paul said, again. His voice soft, almost in a mumble.

A long, uncomfortable moment passed before his mother finally went back to her magazine. I kept staring at Paul then, ready for more adventure. But kept looking down and not at me. Any of my other summer-camp friends would've looked at me with a sly smile before mimicking her as soon as she looked away. But Paul didn't, just kept looking down.

This is where my memory gets slippery. Paul sat in the lake's shallows, digging a hole where the lake met the shore, scooping up the gritty sand with his bare hands to make his own mini lake to rule over. So, I remember him as King Paul. I also remember him as a prisoner. Was he both? Or was he all of it: frog, shark, king, a prisoner to his fleshy kin, a submarine sinking?

Whatever he was, he'd changed, and I didn't understand how to change him back. There had been something powerful in that moment with his mother, a treacherous spell. I didn't understand, then, how shame tips us all over. It's visceral, paralyzing, really. I didn't understand, then, how Paul must've felt having me witness a private piece of his life he didn't want me, a mermaid, to see.

But this story isn't about Paul. It's about me. I stayed in the lake and did handstands, hoping to impress him again. Each time I surfaced he was digging. He didn't look up. He didn't look back at me. I swam back out to the dock and tried not to watch him, but he was creating a glorious mountain next to his mini lake. I swam back in towards the shore and, waist deep, spun in dizzy circles, my arms out like an airplane's so I feel the quiet slip and slap of water. I'd spin faster and faster and then fall into the lake as the sky turned in similar spinning circles. He had both of his feet sunk deep in his watery crater.

Silence is a delicate thing and yet it's so damn difficult to break. I think I wanted to help him cover his legs, planting him deep, pretending he was stuck for good only to and pull him out and save him. Or else I wanted to scoop out my own hole beside his, or have him to join me back in the lake. Whatever it was, it didn't matter to him. He never once looked back at me. It was as if we'd never met, never pretended to be fish or magic.

I sat on the shoreline a couple of yards away from Paul and started scooping up my own damp sand, not with vigor or with a plan but with a halfhearted interest, studying the flecks of mica glinting in the sun, thinking about diamonds and fool's gold. The beach was getting busy, and there wasn't really room for me to dig much anyway. Paul must've felt this, too, since from the corner of my eye I watched him stand up, pull his feet out of his watery hole, and walk to the wharf where he'd showcased his belly flops. He didn't jump or dive or flop back into the lake. He just sat there, dangling his feet in the lake. Another boy I didn't know sat down beside him, and Paul, who was no longer talking to me or even looking at me, smiled at the other boy. Then, they started talking and laughing like nothing else mattered.

I felt something I couldn't identify—jealousy, possessiveness, indignance that I'd been replaced. I dropped the wet sand I'd been holding and stood up fast, which made me feel woozy from the sun. Only then, in that moment, I'd thought I was woozy from Paul's unfaithfulness. I went to the two boys and sat on the other side of Paul, King Belly Flopper, so that the three of us were a row on the wharf's edge, dipping and kicking our feet in the water. But we were not three friends together. The two boys continued talking, ignoring me. The two boys smiled and laughed like they'd always known each other, maybe they had, but I felt outside of it all, unable to find my way back in. It was finding that my gills had closed. It was forgetting there were underwater villages I could dream to explore with strange creatures I could name. It was being out over my head and forgetting how to swim.

It's easy now to see how and why it all happened. I couldn't have put it into words then, but I understood even at that young age that there was an ease about how boys forgot about girls, and I never saw consequences for any boy's ease. Even now, rage overtakes me when I'm around any boy or man who chooses to cruelly dismiss a girl. I'm more sophisticated in how I handle it today, but then, that morning, what else could I do? I was a child, all instinct and attitude.

Sitting next to those boys, being invisible to their private-boy world, I was overcome by the impulse to be noticed, to not be ignored. I wanted there to be consequences for them pretending I wasn't there. Without saying anything to either boy, I slapped Paul as hard as I could on his pale, boney back. I didn't feel good about it, but I couldn't help it, either. It was primal. It was a slap like the slap when he'd belly flopped into the water. It was like laughing at Michael Hayes even when if felt bad to do so.

"What'd you do that for?" he asked, finally looking at me for the first time since his mother had yelled at him. Was it pain or surprise on his face?

I had no answer for him. How could I explain what didn't yet make sense in my child mind? My heart was pounding, and staring at Paul staring at me didn't make me feel better. I didn't know how to get back to how we were earlier, so I did the only physical thing that felt possible. I slapped him again, though the slap was weaker because my muscles felt shaky.

Paul just kept staring at me, and even though I'd wanted him to look at me, it was all wrong. All I could do was jump back into the water—it was a giant jump, a show-off frog jump with a fine splash. I swam back out to the floating dock where he, according to his mother, couldn't go. On the floating dock, I lay belly down with my head turned away from the shore. There was the other side of the lake to think about. The older kids swam there. It didn't seem so far.

Everyone saw me hit the boy. Or I figured they must've. I thought about that, wondered why the adults didn't say anything, why they didn't yell after me. Was I so inconsequential that a slap or two didn't matter? To me, it mattered. I worried that there was an incomprehensible meanness inside of me that could pop up like a jerked knee. I felt out of control and disgusted with myself—feelings I'd thankfully grow out of—and wished I had superhero powers to blend in with the dock so it'd look like I vanished, or maybe push back time and erase or change my actions.

Holding my body perfectly still, then, feeling the sun dry and bake my skin, I understood sunbathing for the first time. Lying there, I thought about tan lines, how the sun could change me if I held still long enough. I fell asleep thinking this, believing in my need to change. I fell asleep rocked by the water moving against the dock, lulled by the sun's heat and grand promises.

Later that summer, I would swim to the lake's other side with my friend Julie and her older sister. The other side wasn't as nice as ours. It didn't have a beach, and the rocks were slimy from disuse. But there were turtles. And the knowledge that I wasn't useless. I told them about the stupid boy Paul who said I couldn't do a mermaid dive or stand on my hands, and so I hit him—rightfully so. They agreed I'd been right, and we laughed. We made up more stories for each other, each funnier than the last, before swimming back to our summer-camp homes.

Wen-Shing Ho

Wild Ginger on the Rock

Act I

In the early days of May, over a year had passed since my father's departure from the Saha world. As Labor Day approached, my husband, Yuzhe, our twelve-year-old daughter Hayen, and I embarked on a journey into the Wuyi Mountains resort district in Fujian, China. This was our first holiday following the COVID-19 isolation and fever waves, and it felt like a much-needed escape. Families from all over were yearning to be free from the virus and the shackles of lockdown restrictions, and they flooded the roads in pursuit of this newfound freedom.

The journey to reach our destination was a long and challenging one. Covering over 1,700 kilometers in six days and five nights, we made the most of the toll-free highways. Yet, our path was marred by frequent car accidents and traffic jams every 100 kilometers.

Finally, we arrived at our lodge on the second day. The fatigue from the journey was palpable. It was a stark contrast to the images we had seen on the booking website. The lodge was far humbler than expected, a reminder of the uncertainties of traveling during peak holiday season. Hotel rooms were in high demand and three times more expensive than standard rates, from five-star accommodations to remote mountain air bed and breakfast rooms. The nonrefundable policy and the soaring demand for rooms had left us with no choice but to accept what we had for a three-day and two-night stay.

Unfamiliar with the region and the newfound COVID-free phenomenon, we found sidewalks teeming with people, parking lots packed to capacity, and were forced to follow traffic for more than two kilometers from the entrance of the Wuyishan National Nature Reserve. The long-distance parking lot was an open field with sand and clouds of dust, lacking temporary pavement for the holiday crowd. As we reached the gate, we joined millions of tourists, young and old, with little ones in tow, only to discover that all the tickets for the popular bamboo raft drift along the Nine-Bend River were sold out for the next three days.

Hayen's initial excitement gave way to disappointment, and she turned to me with a hopeful look in her eyes. "Mama, maybe if we offer more money for a private tour, they might have some extra tickets," she suggested. Amid the holiday chaos, I approached a ticket officer while searching my phone for alternative options.

"No, all package tickets are sold out. Would you like to purchase trolley tickets to explore the park instead?" the ticket officer replied. Reluctantly, I agreed, and as we rode the trolley, Hayen gazed longingly at the passengers on the bamboo rafts, envisioning the wonders of the journey she was missing.

Her yearning couldn't be contained, and soon, she hopped onto one of the bamboo rafts moored by the riverbank, reveling in the motion of the water.

"Hey, get out of the raft!" one of the raftsmen shouted, blowing his whistle. I approached him and inquired about last-minute ticket options. With a gesture, he directed us to a resort hotel near the entrance, where we eventually secured three tickets for 850 Chinese yen. These tickets would grant us passage on an ancient bamboo boat for a journey down the stream.

Once on the raft, I extended a generous tip of sixty Chinese yen to each of the raftsmen, expressing my gratitude for their exceptional service. Their warm smiles spoke of their anticipation for the journey ahead.

Act II

The Nine-Bend River welcomed us with its gentle murmur, guiding our bamboo raft through the enchanting landscape. Our craftsmen, seasoned guides of this mystical realm, began to recite the lyrics of those nine songs, seven-word, four-line idioms.

As we meandered down the winding river, I spotted a solitary wild ginger flower in full bloom, delicately perched on a barren, near-vertical rock, which brought back memories of my father—a cherished recollection from my college days in Taipei nearly twenty years ago.

Back then, as a student, I had journeyed from Kaohsiung in southern Taiwan to the bustling city of Taipei for my education. My father, driven by unwavering love, had embarked on an overnight drive spanning more than 360 kilometers to pay me his first visit. That visit had unexpectedly turned into a road trip and was the first time we had spent together since I was twelve years old in junior high school.

Back then, I knew nothing more than to please my parent by cultivating the books, practicing exams, and memorizing textbooks. "What a waste of my youth!" I thought to myself today. Little did I know that this voyage would transform into a cherished memory, painted with the golden hues of nostalgia.

In that reminiscence, I saw him again—my Papa, a man whose earthly journey had ceased but whose presence had returned to grace my dreams. Papa and I loved the challenge of driving on muddy, rocky roads and hiking for hours in the green forest, listening to the birds, crossing bridges, and resting by waterfalls casting rainbows. That had been our cherished tradition. On that visit to my college, we journeyed to Sanxia's Manyueyuan (full Moon) National Forest Recreation Park where wild ginger flowers adorned sandstone shale trails. It was springtime, and I was intoxicated by the fragrance, with innocent white flowers among the lush green. I couldn't help but exclaim, "Papa, look at those lovely wild ginger flowers leaning on the slopes."

With scissors in hand, he bravely ventured down steep slopes to gather a bouquet of wild ginger flowers for me, surprising me greatly. The memory of him climbing down and returning with that bundle of flowers is etched deep within me, still making my heart skip a beat. I was enchanted by the pure white beauty and fragrant scent of those flowers, which graced my dormitory with their warm aroma and their profound elegance. As I gazed at the fresh-looking wild ginger flower on the distant rock, tears welled in my eyes.

The wild ginger flower seemed to beckon, and in my mind's eye, I saw my father approaching it. "Papa, be careful, it's slippery out there," I whispered, tears flowing freely. That visit with Papa had transformed into an unexpected road trip, a rare opportunity for us to forge bonds through shared experiences. This voyage crystallized into a cherished memory. I felt his presence beside me, and a white crane glided grace-fully over the river, symbolizing peace and grace.

Hayen, with a mischievous glint in her eye, called out to my husband, "Papa, look at the Great Peak. What do you see? It resembles the head with a bright smiling face of our raftman." With a flourish, the raftman paused his oar, allowing the river to cradle us gently as we contemplated the majesty before us.

"Each rock had its appearance and a drama, made up of thirty-per-cent reality and seventy-percent imagination," Yuzhe replied with a grin.

As we continued our journey, the raftsman pointed ahead and said, "Now we are entering the Jade Girl Peak. Can you see the king's daugh-ters? The best spot for a family photo." The three of us held hands, bal-anced our bodies, and walked towards the end of the raft.

"Kimchi!" we said, and the words echoed back. Hearing the bounc-ing back words, we no longer made faces for our photo but looked into the caves surrounding in all directions.

Further along our journey, the raftmen's tour continued to captivate our imaginations.

"We are heading towards the Brazil Amazon River," one of them ex-claimed, his voice brimming with excitement. The tuffs and greens stood above the water symmetrically, with their reflections shifting and chang-ing with each passing moment. We marveled at the rock formations, their shapes reminiscent of distant lands and exotic places.

"Mama! Listen to those children playing in the water by those enor-mous rocks." Hayen, with her both hands, touched my face gently and smiled.

The other raftman chimed in, "Yes. That's the well-known Sydney Opera House in Australia. The noises of water splashes and laughter are musical." He laughed heartily, his enthusiasm contagious.

"Traveling through the Nine-Bend River in Wuyi mountains, you tour around the world," Hayen concluded, shifting her gaze toward my husband and me as we approached the end of our journey.

We all clapped in appreciation for the raftmen's wonderful ride along the river flanked by cliffs. Their tricks had transformed our ordinary excursion into an extraordinary adventure. The ninety-minute raft drift seemed like a glance at the wild ginger flower on the rock, kissed by the breeze.

Act III

As the sun descended, we lingered by the bend for a long while, saluting all the rafts lining up and heading toward the end of Stream Bend. Hayen's eyes filled with amazement and appreciation. On the way to the parking lot, we encountered a local fruit seller carrying his two buckets of green mangos on two ends of a bamboo stick. He cut the fruit on the spot and invited us to taste it.

"It's fresh," Hayen began, and waited for approval to purchase such sweet fruit. I could see the delight in her eyes, and her enthusiasm was infectious.

"Ladies, look at its green color; there are no chemicals injected into the fruit, right?" my husband Yuzhe nodded in agreement, a sign of happiness.

"Yes, we should buy some. I don't mind carrying it," I replied.

Hayen beamed with pride as she held the sweet mangos. "The best way to recall this trip is to have such a souvenir."

We were liberated.

Jean Dowdy

The Shape of Forever

Time is a circle . . . and every circle eventually must close.
—*Anthony Doerr,* Cloud Cuckoo Land

Cade Weaver's construct of time up to this particular moment has been of a nature strictly linear and fairly devoid of emotional embellishment. Calendars and daybook planners, after all, do a fine job marching one through ruler-straight trajectories of days, weeks, and months—all framed in sensible blocks and rectangles and usually in shades of black and white. Cade Weaver is not the sort to be without her daybook.

But, here and now in the curtain-cooled immediacy of her cousin's sickroom, Cade finds the morning's passage wrapped in a sense of something more round and softer, somehow; a bubble of vigil that gently swells and contracts with both the ticking of the mantel clock and the rise and fall of cousin Lulu's measured breaths. Outside, the summer sun itself is easing over the marsh in tiny advances and retreats, fits and starts—its arc now more in sync with the irregular pulse of the lapping river tide than its usual lockstep across a late August sky.

Cade had taken advantage of the clement pre-dawn coolness to walk the five shoreline miles between her house and the cabin Lulu and her husband Jake have been restoring over the last twenty years. A work of sure art wrought through Jake's woodworking genius and Lulu's artistic sensibilities, their cottage is truly a model of appropriate and beautiful small-home-crafting. Or it *would* be, Cade sometimes thinks uncharitably, if these folks could ever just finish the job. Because honestly! How anyone might choose to live amidst so much plaster dust and wood shavings and site sketches scattered about for all these years is simply beyond reason.

In this bedroom-turned-spotless sickroom, though, Jake's tenderness towards his wife is manifest in the scrubbed gleam of the wide-planked pine floorboards, the brushed whiteness of the coverlet cocooning Lulu's resting form, that solitary sea oat stalk in a cut-glass vase by the bed. Jake steps into the room with two steaming mugs of tea, doubly strong and sweet as usual and filled to the rim with hot milk. After lowering the window blind against the late morning sun, he sinks to the floor next to Cade's rocking chair.

"The tumor now appears to be pressing against the frontal lobe," Jake says, and Cade feels the cadence of her pulse slow and swell to the shape of the orb of time-which-is-not-time that has swallowed this room. "Surgery may still be an option," he continues, "but consciousness certainly doesn't appear to be."

Lulu's descent into catatonia had been a slow and deliberate slide, marked initially by an over-obsession with reasoning detail, her speech twisting into loops of insistent phrase. Jake now says that she hasn't spoken a word in two or three days *(but how can one keep track of this time?)*, but that her lips move often, forming soft sentences only she might hear. And perhaps it's not that time has come to a *complete* standstill in this small and tended space, but rather has eased them all into a vaguely spherical and buoyant limbo.

"At least there's no pain," Jake adds, ". . . at this point, anyway." And Cade feels her heart break anew at this matter-of-factness. Jake has always been a no-nonsense kind of guy—the voice of calm reason in any given situation—and while his arrival into her cousin's previously solitary and somewhat unrealized life was neither dramatic nor profound, it effected a metamorphosis in Lulu for which Cade will be eternally grateful. She had always considered that the two met and married "late in life"—but it just now strikes her that, though a silver anniversary approaches *(but where has this time gone?)*, marrying just before the age of forty should scarcely qualify as a geriatric union.

"I have a surprise for our anniversary," Cade is startled to hear Jake now say, as if reading her mind. It had always bothered him, he continues, that he couldn't afford a "real" engagement ring at the time of his proposal to Lulu, opting instead for the extra expense to have their wedding bands carefully engraved with a simple twine of ivy, their initials and wedding date scripted inside. But now—finally—he is working with a jeweler friend in honor of this milestone year to craft a thin gold band into which will be set a single garnet, representative not of Lulu's birthdate but of the month they first met, an unseasonably warm January some thirty years before. That auspicious date will be inscribed on the ring's interior, Jake now says, and adds:

"It's the day I knew the circle of my life would be complete."

The combined warmth of Jake's soft voice, that hot sweet tea, and the sun now at noon easing across the garden side of the cottage lulls Cade into a welcome reverie. She remains gently rocking for a few moments before her attention is suddenly drawn to a gold glimmer winking on and off across the bedroom ceiling. Cade leans forward to refocus and sees that an errant sunbeam has sneaked around the half-drawn blind and is now pushing through the faceted bedside glass vase. This prismed ray now shimmers across the wedding band that Lulu has eased off her shrunken finger and is dreamily rolling in small circles across the top of the coverlet, throwing its reflection to and fro across the ceiling.

"I love this ring," Lulu says in a small but clear tone, her eyes closed and her form yet still. "It feels like forever."

Bethany Bruno

Fed to the Gators

The crunching of crispy pine needles beneath my sneakers echoed among the trees. As I trekked through the small, wooded lot beside our home, my older sister, Donna, gripped the chains of her seat swing. She was completely oblivious to her surroundings, which included my random bursts of singing. Her legs dangled above the scuffed grass while she swayed back and forth. The Walkman cassette player clipped to her jeans pocket blared a Stevie Nicks song about white doves.

Mom had instructed Donna to watch me that day while she worked yet another twelve-hour shift at Hollywood Memorial Hospital. Donna huffed and whined as usual. She claimed to have more important things to do than watch her obnoxious younger sister. "Mom, I'm almost twelve," I said as my cheeks reddened from a mixture of anger and embarrassment. "I don't need a babysitter!"

Mom pulled out the last hot hair curler from her bangs and threw it onto her vanity. She turned her attention back toward us and said through gritted teeth, "It's not up for discussion." Donna stomped away, then slammed her door for good measure. Mom sighed and rubbed her temples. She pulled the front door closed and blew me a kiss through its circular window. "Be a good girl!"

Donna finally came out of her room around noon after I had spent the entire morning watching MTV. The new Flock of Seagulls music video was making me nauseous from all the spinning when she tossed a candy bar into my lap. "After you eat your lunch, we're going outside," she ordered. After I unwrapped my "lunch" and devoured it in three bites, she slid open the sliding glass door and walked into our unenclosed backyard. Aside from the swing set, all we had in our backyard was grass and a few thick Sabal palmetto trees.

Most of our neighbors had perfect square yards that were surrounded by a chain-link fence. When our parents bought the house the year prior, our dad said we would get ours enclosed soon. "But you said we could get a dog," I said, pouting.

Dad shook his head and laughed. "*And* we will, once my new paychecks start rolling in."

Later that week, Mom entered the living room from our patio sliding glass door. "Mike!" she called out, interrupting my slotted personal television time on Saturday mornings. My mother waved my father toward the sliding glass door as he poked his head into the living room. "I was just cautioned by one of our neighbors to have a fence put up as soon as possible." She pointed to our grassy, flat backyard that connected to a wooded lot. "Alligators have walked from the inlet across the street and right into our backyard!"

My ears perked up at the mention of the legendary creatures. I jumped up from the couch and stood at the sliding glass door beside my father and worried mother. "Where are the gators? I don't see—"

"You won't be seeing any in our backyard, that's for sure," she snickered. She locked the door and closed the curtain. With solemn eyes, she looked down at me. "You're to stay away from the inlet. This isn't a zoo. Gators have been known to eat dogs, cats, and whatever else is within their reach. Tell her," she said while nudging my father.

Dad nodded in agreement before saying, "Your mother's right." He then placed a hand on her shoulder. "I will call the fencing company tomorrow. Okay?" Her anxious frown began to dissipate. My dad kissed her forehead. "Our children will be safe, Lisa. I promise."

But that promise died the day a drunk driver ran a red light in Miami and plowed straight into my dad's car. His neck broke instantly. Now, nearly a year later, our backyard is still wide open. The dog collar with our new address on it that I had bought in anticipation of the arrival of my new pet was gathering dust in my closet. Our mom was working long hours—nearly six days a week—just to keep up with the staggering house payments. Donna stayed locked in her bedroom most days. Her headphones seemed glued to her ears; she was always blaring music and ignored everyone and everything. Every day since my dad's death, I have silently wished we had never moved.

I weaved around the trees as I carefully sidestepped the huge spider webs and suspicious clusters of pinecones that probably hid snakes or other bite-happy animals. I could still hear the creaking of our rusted swing set, which told me I hadn't traveled too far. I whacked the foliage around me, pretending the large stick in my hand was a machete slicing through jungle vines. Up ahead was a shallow stretch of swale before the ample inlet.

The swale was home to a variety of wildlife, like snapping turtles and minnows. Iguanas perched themselves all over the hanging branches close to the water. During that summer, I'd come to the swale every day to play my favorite game, "eye spy iguanas." Searching for the reptiles among the greenery proved to be a fun challenge. I felt safer standing by the swale rather than the shoreline of the inlet, where alligators might be lurking. Although I had not yet seen one in the wild, I secretly hoped to do so before the start of the sixth grade in August.

During this time, in addition to the dangerous wildlife of Florida, everyone was on high alert over "stranger danger." Last summer, six-year-old Adam Walsh was kidnapped and brutally murdered. While shopping with his mom at the Hollywood Mall, he spotted the new Atari system on display. He played "Star Master" on a joystick while his mother shopped for a new lamp shade at the nearby Sears. When she returned to the display, little Adam was nowhere to be found. For two weeks, his disappearance was national news as search parties roamed across South Florida. A photo of Adam, missing several teeth and dressed in his white and red minor league baseball uniform, was plastered all over Hollywood. The search was sadly called off when his severed head was discovered over a hundred miles away. What happened to the rest of his body was the subject of rumors. Most people accepted one particular alligator-related speculation as fact.

The first time I heard the rumor was one afternoon when I went grocery shopping with my mom at Publix. My mom turned the cart toward the frozen food aisle while I stayed back to inspect what bag of chips I wanted for the week. A middle-aged man with thick Coke-bottle glasses and a gut that drooped over his pants approached me. With two varieties of chip bags in each hand, he said, "Hey, sweetie. Can you help me for a moment?" I nodded. He smiled. "Which bag do you think my little girl would like best?" As I pointed toward the BBQ chips, my mother's cart swung back into the aisle. Her eyes were wild as she raced toward me.

The man turned on his heel, dropped both bags of chips back onto the shelf, and walked away. When she reached me, she grabbed my wrist and yanked me to her side.

"Oww! Mom, you're hurting—"

"What did I tell you? *NEVER* talk to strangers! Do you want to be cut up into a million pieces and fed to the gators like that Walsh boy?"

With warm, salty tears streaming down my face, I shook my head and mumbled a "no" as she pushed us toward the checkout. After we loaded up the trunk with our groceries, she didn't speak to me once on the drive home. Later that night, once I crawled underneath the sheets, she stood in the doorway and apologized. "I wasn't mad at you, baby. I was mad at myself for letting you out of my sight." She sighed and shook her head, as if shaking off her regret. "I will always protect you, but I can't hold your hand forever. As much as I would love to." She smiled, then stepped inside and sat at the edge of my twin sized bed. "My mother used to tell me, 'The scars of some are warnings to all.' It means that when bad things happen to others, like what happened to that poor little boy, it's our responsibility to ensure the same thing doesn't happen to our loved ones. Monsters live in the shadows, but sometimes they're walking beside us in the light." I nodded, though I didn't fully understand what she was talking about. "Just promise me you'll be more careful when I'm not around. Okay?"

"Okay."

As she reached for the lamp's pull chain, she leaned down to kiss my forehead. "I love you." I drifted off to sleep and dreamed of monsters hiding in darkened corners, waiting for their moment to pounce on me. When I woke up the next morning, while trying to recall my nightmare, I couldn't remember if they ever did.

Dad died soon after that day, sending her overprotectiveness toward me into overdrive. I couldn't go anywhere without Donna or my mom nearby—which is why I was grateful for a moment alone by the swale. I bent down to watch the minnows flapping when I sensed movement to my left. I turned my head and saw a tall man dressed in a tattered and faded Miami Dolphins t-shirt with dark jeans. He looked to be in his thirties, maybe younger. His thick, dirty blonde hair grazed the bottom of his earlobes.

I stood back up and kept my sight locked on him. "Hey, come over here," he ordered. I remained frozen in place. "You're not allowed out here. This is my property." Fearing that I was in trouble, I looked through the woods for the sight of Donna on the swing. Her headphones were still plastered to her ears, so she wouldn't hear me if I called out from here.

"I'm sorry, sir. I didn't know," I said. As I took a step back, he stepped forward.

"You need to come with me. If you don't, I'll call your parents and tell them you were trespassing." He extended his open right hand toward me, beckoning me to grab it. Above each knuckle was a tattooed letter: *T I V E*.

My heart pounded frantically. It was in perfect rhythm with the overflow of thoughts that swirled in my mind. He could've been telling the truth. Or it was all a lie to lure me in. *Either way, you're in trouble*, my mind argued. *Don't be stupid. Run!* Then, as if my mind blew a whistle, I turned and sprinted. My hands were up, gliding back and forth as I darted around trees and brush. Behind me, I could hear his footfalls as he chased. I silently prayed the man wasn't already within arm's reach of me. My hair whipped my back as I leapt over fallen tree trunks. The thuds of his footfalls became louder with each of my desperate strides toward the swing set and Donna.

When the opening to the lot came into view, I waved my arms and screamed. "Donna!" My next cries were cut short by the man's abrupt contact with my back. "Don—"

I fell to the ground below with an oomph, slamming my chin into the dirt. I rolled over and leaned onto my elbows. I began crab walking backwards as I looked up at the man now looming over me like a monster over his prey. Gulped cries erupted from me when the man placed his left hand into his pocket.

He pulled out a knife and revealed another four tattooed letters: *F U G I*. "If you scream again, I'll cut you." He made an upward motion with the knife. "Up." I slowly rose. As soon as I stood upright, he grabbed the collar of my t-shirt and pushed me forward. I placed my hand over my mouth to prevent my screams from emerging. He leaned into my side and whispered "walk" into my ear.

The adrenaline coursing through my veins grew with each step closer to the swale. When we reached the waterline, he released my shirt, causing me to stumble. "Turn around," he ordered. When our eyes made contact, he smiled. "Good girl. Now, you're going to do *exactly* what I say and when I say it. If you do, I'll let you go home." He tilted his head to one side as if gauging my reaction. "Nod if you understand." I nodded, sniffling. He placed the knife back in his pocket before placing both hands on his belt. He unbuckled it, placing both tattooed hands together to form the word *"FUGITIVE."*

My "fight or flight" response ignited as he pulled the belt free from its straps with a whir. I knew I couldn't outrun him, let alone fight him. I had no weapons or anything I could use to protect myself with. I peered around at my surroundings. There was the swale, the woods, and the inlet to my right. My only viable option was the inlet. If I jumped in, I could swim with the current until I reached one of the many shallow docks. He reached for the top button of his jeans. *Now Steph!* My legs uprooted. I ran toward where the ledge of solid land met the water and jumped. All was silent before my body splashed into the murky water.

Once my head broke the surface, I heard his screams from behind me at the shore. My arms and legs propelled me forward through the uncertain waters ahead. Behind me was danger, but what if it was also ahead? Then, another unexpected scream erupted behind me. "Steph!" I turned my head toward the hoarse voice to find Donna standing near the man with panicked eyes. The man lunged for her, grabbing her by the neck before poking the knife delicately into her cheek.

As blood pooled around the blade's tip, I gasped. "Stop! Please, stop!" I turned around in the water and held up my hand in surrender. "I'll come out."

Donna shook her head and pleaded, "No!"

The man removed the knife from Donna's cheek but kept it close. I paddled slowly back toward the shore. His grip was still tight around the back of her neck as he walked them both closer to the shoreline.

I paddled slowly toward them as tears of helplessness took hold. I was swimming toward not only my possible death but now Donna's as well. "Hurry up!" he shouted. When my feet touched the ground below the water, I stopped.

"Steph." She paused. "Don't." Donna pleaded with glassy eyes that begged me to swim back to save myself. But I couldn't leave her at his mercy. Instead, I dragged myself out of the water and plopped down onto the dry dirt surrounding the water's edge.

Suddenly, he released Donna's neck and threw her down beside me. She yelped as her body landed with a thud. We scrambled a few feet away from the man, trying to put some distance between us and him. He smiled, then laughed, shaking his head in delight. He stepped a few feet in front of us, with his back toward the inlet. The man unlaced his boots and kicked those to the side. Next, he unbuttoned his pants and motioned for me to come closer. "It doesn't bite," he laughed.

A scaly, armored predator leaped out of the water in a flash. It was a modern-day dinosaur with its short legs, muscular tail, and long, rounded, toothy snout. Before the man could turn around, the alligator opened its mouth wide, tilted its head sideways, and chomped down on the man's left calf. Both Donna and I drew back onto our elbows, unable to take our gaze from the horrific scene before us. He fell face first into the dirt with a disorienting scream. The alligator began thrashing its intended prey. As the man's torso swung left and right, he released the knife. He clawed at the ground frantically as he peered up at us for help.

The alligator rolled multiple times, causing the man's body to bend at unnatural angles. With no way out, he was at the creature's cold-blooded mercy. The man's wild movements began to slow, and the alligator dragged his defeated body into the water. Donna and I watched, frozen in place, as both man and animal slowly submerged into the darkened water below. As the bubbles and splashes drifted further down the inlet, we turned toward each other with gaping mouths. We quickly grasped hands and pulled each other off the ground before jogging back home through the woods. Between rapid breaths, I asked, "What do we do?" She didn't respond. "Should we call the cops?"

When we entered the perimeter of our backyard, she stopped abruptly and grabbed my shoulders to face her. "We can't tell mom," she said.

"If she finds out, she'll freak and never let either one of us out of her sight for the rest of our lives." I recalled my mom's words that night before bed— 'The scars of some are warnings to all.' Donna's brow furrowed, waiting for my response. "Okay?"

If we called the police, they would show up to collect what's left of the man and kill the gator. After losing our dad and having nearly lost both of her daughters, mom would be paralyzed with fear forever. Ultimately, nothing good comes from calling. And what if we don't call? Well, nothing changes. The things that happened will always be a part of Donna's and my life. No one, not even the police or our mother, can erase those terrifying moments near the inlet. But we can take solace in knowing the monster who walked among us is gone, destroyed by the monster hidden in the dark. I extended my arms and wrapped them around Donna's torso. She hesitated briefly before resting her chin on my head.

I closed my eyes, sighed, then nodded. "Okay."

Anderson Roeth

White Tiger

Back when I was a younger man, I used to hunt deer and elk in the woodland hills of Kentucky. My grandpapa was a long hunter, you see. The man loved the wilderness more than he loved any woman. Before he disappeared out near the Kentucky River, he taught me his craft. I always enjoyed the smell of the woods, the feeling of being under God's good heaven, and the patient stalking of a challenge. Among my friends, I had a good reputation for my hunting skills, having been trained by a well-known long hunter and having used those skills often enough since. One day a friend of mine visited me and my mama down near Hiseville.

"Aug," he said to me (that being short for Augustus, the rather grand name my mother chose for me, I've always felt in mockery of my apparently over-educated, absent father). "Aug, I've heard a tale from a settlement northeast a ways, about some animal that's been killing folks."

"That so, Henry?" I replied, puffing on my pipe. "What sort of animal?"

"That's the question, ain't it?" Henry said. "Some folks are saying the creature's a spirit, called upon them by the Creator for some local sin. Others say it's only a mountain lion. And everything in between, of course, you know how people are."

"Nonsense," I said with the confidence of youth. "I never seen a ghost in these parts or any other. I'd stake my bet on a mountain lion or some other natural creature. It's a wild land still, in many ways, despite our civilizing influence."

"That's true, indeed, that's true, Aug." Henry sipped his beer and tapped his foot on the wooden planks of our porch. "To tell the truth, my curiosity's got the better of me—wondering what indeed the creature might be."

"No knowing, Henry, unless you plan to set out and find the thing yourself." I eyed my friend speculatively.

"I'm no hunter, you know that. I *had* heard that some places up that way are offering a reward for killing the thing, whatever it might be. Can't know for sure, of course, but I brought this up 'cause I thought *you* might be interested."

I remained silent a moment, drawing on my pipe and blowing smoke into the fresh afternoon breeze. The warm sunshine fell playfully among the trees. "It'd be a bit of a jaunt," I said, "with no certain guarantee of a worthy end, if you ask me."

Henry nodded my way, agreeing, and continued tapping his foot rhythmically.

After Henry left, disappointed perhaps, I couldn't stop thinking about the creature up northeast, despite my hesitation. Henry had called the thing right: my mind felt aflame with the mysterious possibilities. Ghost, mountain lion, or something else? Some unknown predator that had somehow slipped, unseen, through all the years people had been settling this wide wilderness? The thing weighed on my mind, like a mythical stag in a children's story, ever hunted by ancient kings, always and forever elusive. But I was confident in the skills my grandpapa had imparted to me. I could succeed where forgotten nobility had failed. It wasn't many days before I decided to go looking for it.

I took my time on the journey. The early summer weather was just about as perfect as anyone could ask for. The grass and the leaves on the trees were green and hale, the sunshine was warm, and the sky bright and blue, with bits of white cloud scudding on a high wind. Down among the trees, the breeze rustled through the leaves, until I felt like I walked in an ocean and the tide was rushing around my ears.

On the fourth day out from home, I climbed northward up the back of a densely forested hump, canting upward to an open sky. The paths were few and I made it to the top about midday, huffing and sweating. The ridge was broad and flat until I came to the far edge, where the ground fell steeply away, and I took in the view. The trees were thick, but I could see below me where they circled sharply round a town, a small community called Tin Hook, just what I'd been looking for, having asked several miles back for directions from a farmer. The town was built in a large, cleared patch of ground: a ramshackle collection of wooden houses from which smoke rose, along with one large brick building built on top of a mound at the eastern edge of town. A dirt road ran through it from east to west and ran on in both directions for miles. Westward, I could see lower hills mixed with a few flatter patches, probably outlying farms and homesteads. Above the town to the north, I could see another ridge, almost twin to the one on which I stood, beyond which lay the misty blue horizon. I smiled at the peaceful, idyllic place and made my careful way down the slope before me.

On the south side of Tin Hook stood a large, sprawling building named the Robinson Inn, and I decided to stop in for some rest and information. The matron, a friendly rosy-cheeked woman, showed me into a tidy, but dusty, dining room. I ordered a mug of beer, some bread, sweet potatoes, and venison. Good fare for the morning of exertion I'd had. When she'd set the food on the table, the matron sat down too, the place being empty at the moment save for me.

"Where you headed?" she asked as I bit into the rich, dark bread and washed it down with a swig of beer.

"I don't know for certain, ma'am," I replied. "I came up here from down near Hiseville, couple days walk southeast, looking for the source of some rumors I'd been hearing."

"Oh? What kind a rumors?" she said, though her sharp look made me think she already knew.

"Heard there's a creature or animal, been killing folks."

She frowned, nodding. "There's been something in the area, truth be told. There's the Owens farm up the ridge—lost a few cattle. A bit further north at one of the more isolated homesteads, Mr. Fisher's wife disappeared. Sad, she was mother of several young 'uns. The kids were sent off to stay with their mother's sister up near Louisville. Fisher himself is still up there, stalking about, they say. Here around town, there've been a few stories circulating, about some white shadow, showing up in the dusk-light, wailing up a racket, terrifying folks and disappearing before anyone can even think to shoot at it."

"Any thoughts as to what you think it might be, ma'am?" I asked, between bites.

"It's hard to say," she said. "There's folks who say it's the vengeance of the Lord for sin, that Ms. Owens and Mr. Fisher committed adultery, or some like ugliness. Although I've met the Fishers and the Owens, and I must say none of those folks struck me as the type. They seem like good folks to me."

I chewed thoughtfully for a moment. "Well, innkeeper's well placed to observe folks. I'd bet on your judgment of character, ma'am." The matron smiled at this bit of flattery. "It's more likely just an animal, doing what all animals do to try to survive," I said philosophically.

She held up a finger and wagged it at me, very maternally. "You're probably right, but that doesn't make it any less dangerous going looking for it, up in those hills. You keep your eyes peeled, young man."

I tipped my head respectfully. "Yes ma'am. I'll take all the care in the world."

That afternoon, I asked around, and found out that Ms. Robinson was right. Several people around town had stories about strange occurrences. Every time this white shadow had been seen, it was pretty far outside town, most times around dusk, a few in the dark of night. Not one person was entirely certain of what they saw though, and as no one had been attacked or disappeared this close to town, I resolved to go north the next day and talk to the folks who had a more intimate experience.

The next morning, ragged edged clouds crowded the slowly brightening sky. I threaded my way up the northern ridge in the cool air and soon arrived at the farm Ms. Robinson had directed me towards. The farmer, Mr. Owens, was in the barn hollering at the farmhands when I showed up and knocked loudly on the open barn door. He looked at me in mild confusion and made his way over. Once I had explained myself, he took me to the farmhouse, where Mrs. Owens served us tea while he told me the story. It was short and most of it took place out of the man's sight. What he did confirm was that the cattle were later found, mostly eaten up, and furrowed with ragged claw marks like a poorly plowed field. What was left had already been taken away by the knackers, so unfortunately, I couldn't observe the evidence for myself—but it at least put paid to the ghost idea Henry had floated several days before. By this time, it was nearing lunchtime and Mrs. Owens offered me some cold chicken, cheese, and persimmon pudding. I accepted gratefully. Afterwards, Mr. Owens provided some helpful directions and I continued on my way north to find Mr. Fisher.

The morning clouds had overtaken most of the sky, with only a thin strip of blue remaining near the horizon to the north and the west. One of the Owens's dogs followed me to the edge of the fields north of the farmhouse, as if escorting me off the property. He barked and zipped off back home as soon as I hopped the wooden fence. Fisher's homestead was several miles on from the Owens, set underneath a group of massive trees that looked as old as the hills which rose around them. It was cool and grey beneath the crowns of the trees, spread like a vaulting cathedral roof far overhead. No smoke rose from the chimney, there were no voices to be heard, no tread of boot or other proof of activity. All was silent and dark. As I reached the steps to the porch, a sense of foreboding came over me. I paused for a moment before taking a deep breath and ascending. A knock on the door only increased my uneasiness, as the door was ajar, and swung open further at the touch of my knuckles.

I called out and heard back only a dull, heavy silence. Pushing the door the rest of the way open, I observed a short entrance hall in a state of ruinous destruction. A mirror on the wall was shattered, and below it, a table had been hacked into two splintered halves. A long-handled axe rested between them; its blade bitten deep into the floor. Ceramic shards and soil littered the floor around it like an explosion, and right in the center lay a bedraggled, formerly blood-red flower, scarlet beebalm. Bits of soil led away further into the house. Screwing up my courage, I stepped gingerly through the hall.

The front room was shadowed and dusty, but not destroyed as the entrance hall had been. The blackened fireplace was cold and full of ashes. I did a quick search of the rest of the house and, finding nothing, headed out the back door, glad to be quit of the place. The size of the small house belied the vast emptiness it held, a world of sorrow tangled in its fragile wooden bones. I breathed deeply of the fresh air, tasted leaves and plants, and then a sourness on my tongue. And turned at last to find Mr. Fisher, staring cavernously at me.

I sighed, filled to the brim with the desolation of both the house behind me and the man before me. He was propped up against the wide trunk of one of his beautiful, ancient trees, eyes hooded. Behind the ruined flesh and matted hair of his scalp a dark red sunburst of blood stained the rough bark, vile simulacrum of the exploded pottery and scarlet beebalm in the hall of the house. Across his knees rested a clearly well-kept and polished rifle. He wasn't long dead, for as sour as the air around him was, the stench wasn't what it would become just yet. I removed my hat, bent down before him, and bowed my head in silent prayer.

After a time, I stood and went searching for a shovel. In the waning afternoon light, the strip of sky to the west shooting bright red rays into the grey cathedral beneath the trees, I dug a grave for poor Mr. Fisher. My heart was filled with a confused grief I hadn't often felt in my life, perhaps only akin to the sadness after my grandpapa disappeared. At the time, I had wished I could see a body, if only to say goodbye. Now I was glad I hadn't been subjected to that. I couldn't bear the thought of my grandpapa's eyes, like dark empty windows, filled with the same hollow vacancy contained within Mr. Fisher's body and house.

I went into the house one more time, gently picked up the lifeless scarlet beebalm, and took it out to lay at the head of the grave. Removing my hat once more, I whispered a final prayer over the mound of fresh earth covering Mr. Fisher's earthly remains. Despite the failing dusk beneath the trees, I left that place, hoping never to return. I hoped at the time, and still hope, the man's poor young ones never returned either, for their sakes. I hope they had happy, full lives, filled with love and peace, the emptiness of that house left far behind them. As for me, it felt like a different world than the one in which I had supped on chicken and cheese with the friendly Owens. I made camp in a dell a mile away from the Fisher house, and after a long time staring into the flames of my fire, I finally fell asleep, the adventure turned all to shadow and grief and uncertainty.

A pair of snugly-moccasined feet rested in front of me when I awoke the next morning. I jerked up and reached for my rifle, but my hands closed on nothing but thin air. A Shawnee man sat on a fallen log, cradling my rifle in the crook of his arm. A bow was slung across his back, and a tomahawk hung from a cord at his waist. He smiled lazily at my startled surprise. I froze for a long moment, my heart beating hard and fast, but the man made no move to shoot or otherwise engage me. Not knowing what else to do, I pushed myself to a seated position and hazarded a greeting. "Good morning."

"Good morning," he said politely, his English clipped and precise. "You buried James Fisher."

"Yes, I did," I replied in some consternation. "How'd you know?"

He ignored my question. "Are you a friend of Mr. Fisher's?"

I hesitated, unsure of what kind of situation I had landed myself in. Answering or not answering the man's questions might lead to violence, either way. Since he had my rifle, however, it seemed my choice was taken from me. "I never met the man," I said. "I came looking to talk to him, but it seems I was a bit late for that."

He looked thoughtful for a moment. "If you did not know the man, why did you bury him?"

"I don't know. I felt I couldn't leave the man in such straits," I said honestly. "It was a small kindness." I shrugged to stretch my sore shoulders, which apparently didn't agree on the size of the kindness, especially after my tense night's sleep.

"James Fisher was a friend to me, and my people," the man said sadly. "Thank you for your kindness."

I was taken aback by the unexpected gratitude and found myself not knowing what to say. He sat quietly and looked down at his feet, as if we were paying James Fisher a moment of silent respect. Maybe we were. At last, he looked back up at me. "What did you come to speak to Mr. Fisher about?"

"If you were a friend of Mr. Fisher's, you know his wife disappeared. Taken by a white shadow, the folk nearby say. I was hoping he could give me some idea where she was taken."

The man nodded. "This creature is known to us. It has killed many of my people. It took Fisher's wife, and now Fisher, our only ally in this region. Our hunters, our *prayers*"—he said the word with a peculiar twist—"our spirits, all have fallen silent. There is no reasoning with this creature."

"I don't plan to reason with it," I said.

"It's a dangerous thing you hunt." He looked at me seriously for a long moment. Finally, he gestured towards my pack and my hat, then stood as if to go. "Come," he said and stepped lithely up the northern slope of the dell I had camped within.

"Where you going?" I hollered up at him.

He turned and gestured me to follow. "Come," he said again. Again, I hesitated, but as I was effectively directionless, I decided to give myself up to fate, or the good Lord's plan, whatever was taking place here. I gathered up my pack, jammed my hat on my head, and climbed up the slope behind him.

"Where you taking me?" I asked when I caught up.

He looked at me sideways, a sly smile on his face. "You will see."

We headed due north. The pale light of a cloudy morning filtered softly through the trees, and the air was quiet and still, as if the forest weren't quite awake yet. We hiked through hilly country for about an hour, threading our way through thick brush under maples and hickory trees. At last, we came to a lip that looked down a rocky slope to a number of small structures of some sort. The Shawnee man led the way down to the graves, and I followed slowly. The air felt still and thick at the bottom of the slope. The trees had thinned, and the sun had partially broken through the clouds, falling hot and uncomfortable, like a late summer afternoon come months early. I saw now that the structures were low mounds of fresh earth, topped with layers of poles, then layers of bark, and finally, small wooden grave houses, all oriented from east to west. I sighed and felt a twinge of the confused grief of the day before, reminded of the grave I had so recently dug. My guide watched me closely.

"These all killed by the creature?" I asked quietly. I counted eight graves.

He nodded.

"I'm sorry."

"Thank you." He nodded sadly. "Over the ridge, about a mile to the northeast, that's where we found . . . what remained . . . of one of our people." He pointed to a ridge opposite the one we had just come down. "I will take you there, and then I will go."

"Go?"

"My people are leaving. This place is no longer safe. Even before we had knowledge of Fisher's death, we had considered it." He gestured at the graves as explanation. "There is no reasoning with this creature," he said, as he had before. "I was sent to discuss the issue with Fisher. With his passing, our departure is assured."

We traveled the final mile in companionable silence. Such a little while we had spent together, and yet I felt a strange kinship with this Shawnee, who had known and been friends with a man I had never known, and yet whose passing caused such sadness in me. My young self was troubled by the incompatibility between this feeling of kinship and the stories of savages which I had grown up hearing. I stole a look at him every now and then as we walked, pondering.

After a time, we arrived at a hollow between a small creek and a rock face, probably fifteen feet high, that ran northwest to southeast. The man bent down near a patch of soil and thick grass, a few bushes and a black walnut tree nearby. It wasn't difficult to see the signs. The grass was bent and torn, the ground furrowed and disturbed violently. Dried blood stained the soil and the walnut tree's roots rusty shades of brown. There were a number of footprints, probably of those who found and carried the remains away. Most interesting to me though, was the detritus of moss, twigs, and dead leaves that littered the site.

"This was where we found one of our boys. It was quick. The boy was probably crouched there," The Shawnee man said, pointing to the lip of the hollow. "And was dragged here." I circled the site to the spot above the hollow, and despite a confusion of vague footprints, thought he was probably right. A trail of broken and bent grass and ragged soil led from the spot where I stood down to the center of the bushes where the Shawnee man still crouched.

"Mountain lion," I said. "Were the remains covered with the debris, leaves and such, down there?"

He rose from his crouch as I returned to the kill-site. "Yes, but I tell you, this is no mountain lion. This creature is bigger, more dangerous, and some spirit is within it. Some of our people have caught sight of it, but the thing is swift and always disappears. It may be a foolish thing for you to hunt this creature alone. How will you succeed where our hunters have failed, and our spirits refused to aid us?" He said this without rancor or anger, sincerely concerned, it seemed to me.

I chewed on the inside of my cheek, his words causing fear to rise up in me. "I don't know the answer to that, but something drives me on, hard to say what." Despite my nervousness at his words, I felt that I had to see the hunt through. "Could use your help though."

He shook his head, gravely. "I am sorry, I must meet my people. We travel west." He held out my rifle to me, which I had almost forgotten he had, then he gave me directions to a few of the other kill sites within the surrounding area. "I wish you well," he said at last.

"Thank you," I said, "for all your help. I wish you and your people safe travels." He smiled slyly once more. I hefted my rifle over my shoulder and watched him disappear into the trees. Only after he was gone did I realize I had never even asked his name.

After my erstwhile guide left, a tension grew within my body. After what I'd seen, I began to doubt my own ability to finish this hunt, to find this violent apparition that had so haunted the people in the region. The man had said it truly—if the Shawnee had failed, what hope had I? And yet, something called to me in this forest, like a revelation waiting to be unveiled within my sight, fear mixed with almost-religious ecstasy. Barely discernible tracks left the hollow, big ones, running southeast along the rock face. I followed them, keeping a sharp eye out for further signs. I lost the tracks eventually, but then found a pile of scat, deftly covered, but visible to the trained eye, and then further on, a scraped patch of ground, evidence of a cat marking territory. A very large cat marking territory. I was sweating now as the day grew hotter and the fear I felt continued to mount. The thought occurred to me, if the lion lived near, it might know I was here. My skin crawled at the thought.

By early afternoon, I came across a crevice in the rock face that wound up to the top. With some effort and the removal of my pack, I squeezed through and sat with my back to a flat-sided boulder, my legs hanging down the rock face. I leaned my rifle against the rock behind me, then unpacked some of the chicken and cheese left over from Mrs. Owens' gracious lunch the day before. As I chewed, I studied the view below, hoping for some stroke of inspiration regarding what felt like an increasingly fruitless and dangerous quest. At this point, I still had enough time to get back to any civilized folk before darkness fell. My camp the night before had felt safe enough, but now I felt I was in the lion's den, as it were. I knew from the Shawnee man that there were a few other kill-sites nearby. I could stake one out, but the idea of spending the night near such a sight was terrifying to me now. Increasingly, my confidence in my hunting skill felt more and more foolish, a product of youthful overconfidence rather than the wisdom of experience. The violent death of Mr. Fisher, the Shawnee graves, the warnings I had received from Mrs. Robinson and the Shawnee man—I had to admit that my drive to continue this hunt might have been my own pride. There are some things in the world we cannot fix, some people we cannot save. I leaned my head against the cool rock behind me and eyed the ragged grey dome of sky, like the iron jaws of a trap, overhead.

A loud crack rang out below the rock face, and I jerked awake, disoriented. The daylight was failing, shadows beginning to coalesce beneath the trees. A cold breeze blew through the canopy like eerie whispers. My hand jerked toward my rifle, still leaning against the boulder beside me, but my shoulder tipped it over. In the gloom, I misjudged, my knuckles brushing the forestock just before the rifle clattered over the edge to fall well beyond my reach at the foot of the rock face. I breathed quietly, panic flooding my thoughts.

Anxiously, I searched the growing shadows below for any sign of movement. Between one breath and the next, he suddenly became visible to me, as if he truly was some kind of spirit: a huge white face framed in lines of shadow, his jaws stained red and brown with the blood of his victims. I'd seen paintings of tigers before, but this one wasn't orange like the ones I remembered. He was massive, like a breathing hill three times the size of a mountain lion, white as fresh-fallen snow and striped in blackest shadow. In the waning daylight, his eyes glowed with an aggressive intelligence, a violence somehow both calm and lazy, unconcerned. There was no doubt, his gaze rested squarely upon me. I sat frozen, a weight upon my soul, the anticipated revelation of the morning turned all to incomprehensible terror. He didn't belong here, this alien apparition from some far jungle on the other side of the world. I understood, for a single moment, what it might feel like to see white sails on the seaward horizon or a white face across brown sands.

We faced each other at this distance for what felt like an eternity, my breath raking through my lungs painfully, sweat running down my brow and cooling in the breeze, so that I shivered. I had never felt myself so fragile, so helpless, so at the mercy of another creature. At last, the monster rose, took a last lazy, fire-eyed glance in my direction, yawned and licked his stained chops, then turned to pace northwest along the rock face, eventually dissolving into encroaching shadow.

Whatever power held me motionless released me upon the tiger's leave-taking. It was almost full dark. I did the only thing I could: I left my rifle behind, turned tail and ran southeast along the top of the rock face, until the land sloped down, and I turned south in an attempt to reach Tin Hook as fast as anyone possibly could. I felt I had seen through myself that day, that my worth had been measured and found lacking. Sometimes, there ain't nothing you can do in the face of strength like that monster had in spades, except run. Poor Mr. and Mrs. Fisher are probably looking down at me disappointed, and if so, I can only beg forgiveness. I was a young man, younger than I realized at the time, and I had had enough death and fear, so much that it caught hold of me.

In a trance, I made it to Tin Hook and immediately slept for almost a full day, then slipped out in the early morning so as to avoid questions. A day and a half later, I made it to ol' Louisville, feeling the need to be around civilized strangers, and proceeded to choke down bourbon after bourbon, hoping the touch of death upon my soul would pass. I couldn't understand why the thing had let me live. After three days of solid drinking, I began to come back to myself. Eventually, I headed back south to home, where Henry was sorely disappointed at my failure to provide enough detail to satisfy his curiosity.

To this day, I wonder what became of that ol' tiger. I heard rumors of more deaths in the region for a few years, but a tiger can't live forever. When I would hear them from Henry or someone else, I would just shake my head and sigh, a shame I couldn't face curled up deep inside me. Sometimes I wonder if I really saw him, licking his bloody chops, and yawning, or if I was just tired and heartsore from everything I'd seen. Because people always die, don't they? And we search for a reason to make sense of it all. It's not a tame world we live in.

Some nights in bed, I imagine he didn't let me go after all, that he'll be coming for me one of these days. Some night I'll be sleeping and that big ol' fellow will show up to drag me to my final rest. Aggression like that can't be sated, it gets spread all around, visited on the undeserving and the deserving alike. A tiger can't be anything other than a tiger, now can it? Maybe that tiger'll be prowling around the edges, waiting, come what may.

Cornerstone

poetry by writers K–12

Emma Catherine Hoff

Eyeshadow Bear Coat

The daycare child with the iridescent bear ears
reminds me of my math teacher's green eyeshadow,
which is like a neon sign I can't look away from,
declaring something twisted and yet orderly,
gaudy yet practical. This eyeshadow sees me
and I can't stop staring. It is serious and dressed
in that puffy coat that comes to all children
eventually. And it's the sight of this girl with
eyeshadow and a puffy coat that makes me smile,
look past the other children in the line, and mouth,
hello, Mrs. Bear.

Emma Catherine Hoff

Puglia

1
Water moving   in shimmering folds   but this is from the sun
   up and down   I never liked glitter

2
Drivers don't care   if they hit loud kittens
    that climb up the steps   to beg
      or if they hit   other cars
        backing up   freaking out

3
Jumping
    from the cliff
        landing in the water
           either
           curled up
           like oranges
           or straight
           like shish kebabs

4
Diligent   ants
    communicate   with
      each   of
        their   pals
        before   leaving

5
Salt peels
          off
                your
                      skin
                            after
                                  the
                                        beach
                                              and
you wonder
                      if you're
                                              fall
                                              ing
                                              a
                                              part

Emma Catherine Hoff

Not Enough Duck

A recent visit to The Ellington
        start
             looking at food from a different perspective.

A more serious topic
        caramelized onions
                severely lacking in duck.

Little mountain
        of scallops
            mini garden on the side.

completed with strawberries
            and, of course,
                mint.

I picked up a piece of bread
           and
             tossed almonds scattered all over my plate.

glory of these foods
         makes me start
            ranting.

large jug of olive oil
         next to beautiful
            butter.

chickpea puree
        where grilled octopus sits.
                        surrounded by tomatoes.

my order
        your order
                our order.

No shortage of other ingredients
                        just not enough duck.

Contributors' Notes

Dianne Aprile is an author and editor of books, a poet and essayist whose work has appeared in magazines, journals, anthologies and newspapers. She serves on the faculty of the Naslund-Mann School of Writing, Spalding University, where she has taught creative nonfiction since the program's inception in 2001. A native of Louisville, she was an award-winning journalist for 30 years and, with her husband, owned and operated a jazz club for five years before moving to Washington state. The couple returned to their hometown in 2022.

Pamela Baker (she/her) is a prose writer living in Central Florida. Her stories and essays have appeared in many journals, including *Story*, the *Sycamore Review*, *The Southeast Review*, *Cream City Review*, and *Flyway*, and the *Creative Nonfiction* In Fact Books anthology, *I Wasn't Strong Like This When I Started Out: True Stories of Becoming a Nurse*. She teaches writing and rhetoric at the University of Central Florida.

Susan Campbell Bartoletti has published poetry as well as short stories, picture books, novels, and nonfiction for young readers. Her awards include a Newbery honor, an ALA Robert F. Sibert Award for Nonfiction, the NCTE Orbis Pictus Award for Nonfiction, among others.

Ace Boggess is author of six books of poetry, most recently *Escape Envy*. His writing has appeared in *Indiana Review, Michigan Quarterly Review, Notre Dame Review, Harvard Review,* and other journals. An ex-con, he lives in Charleston, West Virginia, where he writes and tries to stay out of trouble. His seventh collection, *Tell Us How to Live*, is forthcoming in 2024 from Fernwood Press.

Gaylord Brewer is a professor at Middle Tennessee State University, where he founded and for 20+ years edited the journal *Poems & Plays*. The most recent of his 16 books of poetry, fiction, criticism, and cookery are two collections of poems, *The Feral Condition* (Negative Capability, 2018) and *Worship the Pig* (Red Hen, 2020). A book of brief nonfiction, *Before the Storm Takes It Away*, is forthcoming from Red Hen in spring 2024.

Bethany Bruno is an Irish-Italian American writer. She was born and raised in South Florida. She obtained a BA in English from Flagler College and later earned an MA from the University of North Florida. Her writing has been previously featured in several journals, including *The Sun, The MacGuffin, Ruminate, Every Day Fiction, The First Line,* and *Lunch Ticket Magazine*. She lives in Huntsville, Alabama, with her husband and daughter. She's represented by Caitlin Mahoney of the William Morris Endeavor Agency. Her debut novel will be published in 2024. You can find her at www.bethanybrunowriter.com.

Teresa Cader's fourth poetry collection, *AT RISK*, was selected by Mark Doty for the 2023 Richard Snyder Memorial Book Prize and is forthcoming from Ashland Poetry Press in October 2024. Her first book *Guests* (1992) won the Norma Farber First Book Award from the Poetry Society of America and *The Journal* / Charles B. Wheeler Poetry Prize and was published by the Ohio State University Press. Her other award-winning poetry books include *The Paper Wasp* and *History of Hurricanes.* She has won fellowships from the NEA, the Massachusetts Cultural Council, the Bunting Institute-Radcliffe, MacDowell, and Bread Loaf, and her work has been translated into Polish and Icelandic. She lives in Arlington, Massachusetts.

Rebekah Clarkson is a writer living and working on Kaurna and Peramangk lands in South Australia. Her short stories have appeared in publications including *Best Australian Stories* and *Something Special, Something Rare: Outstanding Short Stories by Australian Women* (Black Inc.) and been recognized in awards including the ABR Elizabeth Jolley Short Story Prize, Fish Publishing Short Story Prize and Glimmer Train's Fiction Open. She is the author of *Barking Dogs* (Affirm Press), a critically acclaimed short story cycle set in Mount Barker, South Australia. Rebekah has taught creative writing at several Australian universities, and as a guest lecturer at the University of Texas at Austin and the University of Cambridge.

Jean Dowdy is a displaced Appalachian and hopefully soon-to-be-retiring horticulturalist who lives and works in the relative wilds of northeast Florida. In addition to local gardening columns over the years, her poetry can be found in *Oberon Poetry* and *SWWIM Every Day!* (online)—and the online journal *Salvation South* recently featured both a personal essay and short story.

Kathleen Driskell is an award-winning poet and teacher. She is the author of six books of poetry including *Goat-Footed Gods*, a collection forthcoming from Carnegie-Mellon University Press. Her poems and essays have appeared or are forthcoming in many nationally known literary journals including *The New Yorker, River Teeth, Appalachian Review, Shenandoah, Southern Review, Rattle* and are featured online on *Poetry Daily, Verse Daily*, and in *American Life in Poetry.* Past chair of the AWP Board (2019–22), Kathleen is professor of Creative Writing and Chair of the Naslund-Mann Graduate School of Writing at Spalding University, home of the nationally distinguished low-residency MFA in Writing Program.

Alexander Etheridge has been developing his poems and translations since 1998. His poems have been featured in *The Potomac Review, Scissors and Spackle, Ink Sac, Cerasus Journal, The Cafe Review, The Madrigal, Abridged Magazine, Susurrus Magazine, The Journal, Roi Faineant Press,* and many others. He was the winner of the Struck Match Poetry Prize in 1999, and a finalist for the Kingdoms in the Wild Poetry Prize in 2022. He is the author of, *God Said Fire,* and the forthcoming, *Snowfire and Home.*

Kevin Grauke has published work in such places as *The Threepenny Review, The Southern Review, Quarterly West, Ninth Letter,* and *Cimarron Review.* He's the author of the short story collection *Shadows of Men* (Queen's Ferry Press), winner of the Steven Turner Award from the Texas Institute of Letters. He lives in Philadelphia.

Charles O. Hartman has published eight collections of poetry, including *Downfall of the Straight Line* (Arrowsmith Press, 2024), as well as books on jazz and song (*Jazz Text,* Princeton 1991) and on computer poetry (*Virtual Muse,* Wesleyan 1996). His *Free Verse* (Princeton 1981) is still in print (Northwestern 1996), and *Verse: An Introduction to Prosody* was published by Wiley-Blackwell in 2015. In 2020 he co-edited, with Martha Collins, Pamela Alexander, and Matthew Krajniak, a volume on Wendy Battin for the Unsung Masters series. He is Poet in Residence Emeritus at Connecticut College. He plays jazz guitar.

Dr. Wen-Shing Ho is a renowned filmmaker, writer, and academic, celebrated for her impactful contributions to film, music, and dance. Her film "TAKAO DANCER" (2013) has earned significant acclaim, notably praised by *Variety* for its unconventional narrative technique. This recognition is a testament to Dr. Ho's innovative approach to storytelling, with her work being showcased at esteemed festivals, including the Tokyo International Film Festival, the Hong Kong International Film Festival, and prestigious venues like the Smithsonian in Washington D.C. and the Singapore National Gallery Theater.

In academia, Dr. Ho's dissertation on the musical composition techniques of Maurice Ravel and Toru Takemitsu in the context of digital cinema was selected for inclusion in the LABS Abstract Leonardo database in 2016. Her written works, including "Tear Love Smile" and "Rag and Bone," have received accolades, with the latter earning a Pushcart Prize nomination in 2020. Additionally, she presented her short story and paper "Game-Mode" improvisation: composing short stories with filmed diaries at the 16th International Conference on the Short Story in English in Singapore.

Dr. Ho's educational background includes a Doctor of Science in Screen Expression from Waseda University in Tokyo, Japan, graduate studies in Film Music at Tisch School of the Arts, New York University, and a Master of Fine Arts in Film and Electronic Media from the School of Communications at American University in Washington, DC.

In her professional roles, Dr. Ho has served as an assistant professor at DeSales University, been a pioneer scholar at Nanyang Technological University (2005–2010), and acted as an associate researcher at Waseda University (2013–2014). Currently, she holds the position of a tenured associate professor at the University of Southern California and the Shanghai Jiao Tong University Joint Institute of Cultural and Creative Industry in Shanghai, China. Dr. Ho's influential work spans filmmaking, academia, and creative expression, solidifying her as a notable figure in the global arts and culture landscape.

Michael Jackman is a published poet and a singer/songwriter and multi-instrumentalist (guitar, dobro, flute, pennywhistle) who lives in New Albany, Indiana. He is a retired senior lecturer of writing at Indiana University Southeast. He now writes, maintains a small homestead with his wife and son, and performs music locally, most often with his Louisville-based band Crazy Chester. He is the author of the chapbook *Letters from Spickert Knob* (Marian University) and the article "Metre and meaning in Jane Kenyon's 'Song'" (*New Writing: The International Journal for the Practice and Theory of Creative Writing*).

Rob MacDonald lives in Boston and is the editor of *Sixth Finch*. Some of his poems can be found in *Fou, Gulf Coast, jubilat, The Adroit Journal, Washington Square Review* and other journals. He is the author of *Situation Normal* (Rye House Press) and *Resuscitation Party* (Racing Form Press).

Elizabeth Majerus's chapbook, *Songs Are Like Tattoos*, is available from Finishing Line Press. Her poems have appeared in journals including *The Madison Review, Rhino Poetry,* and *Pangyrus*. She lives in Urbana, Illinois, with her family and is one-third of the band Motes. elizabethmajerus.wordpress.com

Kevin McLellan is the author of *Sky. Pond. Mouth.* (winner of the 2024 Granite State Poetry Prize selected by Alexandria Peary); *in other words you/* (winner of the 2022 Hilary Tham Capital Collection selected by Timothy Liu); *Ornitheology; Tributary; Round Trip* and the book objects, *Hemispheres* and [*box*] which reside in several special collections including the Blue Star Collection at Harvard University. Kevin also makes videos which have appeared in the Berlin Short Film Festival; Flickers' Rhode Island Film Festival; the International Festival of Winter Cinema; the LGBTQ+ Los Angeles Film Festival ("Dick" won Best Short Form Short); Nature & Culture Film Festival; the Vancouver Queer Film Festival and others. They live in Cambridge, Massachusetts. kevmclellan.com/

Derek Mong is the author of three poetry collections from Saturnalia Books—*Other Romes*, *The Identity Thief*, and *When the Earth Flies into the Sun* (October 2024)—as well as a chapbook, *The Ego and the Empiricist*, from Two Sylvias Press. Individual poems, essays, and translations have appeared widely: the *LA Times*, the *Boston Globe*, the *Kenyon Review*, *Blackbird*, *Free Inquiry*, *Pleiades*, *Verse Daily*, and the *New England Review*. He and his wife, Anne O. Fisher, received the Cliff Becker Translation Award for *The Joyous Science: Selected Poems of Maxim Amelin* (White Pine Press). They also co-edit the literary journal *At Length*. From 2008–2010, Derek served as the Axton Fellow in Poetry at the University of Louisville. He and his family currently live in Indiana, where he chairs the English Department at Wabash College.

Alan Naslund began his education and interest in poetry in grade school by attending the one-room, country school, North Yantic, in Blaine County, Montana, near Chinook, Montana, where Friday afternoon programs included recitation of memorized poems. He has received BA and MA degrees from the University of Montana and a Ph.D. from the University of Louisville—each degree in studies of English Language and Literatures. Writing awards he has won include a Kentucky Arts Council Al Smith Fellowship in Fiction, a Sewanee Writers Conference Tennessee Williams Fellowship in Playwriting, a Vermont Studio Center fellowship in fiction, a national award in poetry from *The Louisville Review*, and an award in playwriting from the University of Montana. Alan Naslund is the author of *Silk Weather* (Fleur de Lis Press), and a novel, *Hob's Way*, an ebook available on Amazon.

Dr. Emily Jane O'Dell is the author of *The Gift of Rumi: Experiencing the Wisdom of the Sufi Master* (St. Martin's Press) and a professor at Parami University in Myanmar. Stateside, she has taught at Columbia, Brown, and Harvard, where she received a teaching excellence award, and she has also been a Research Fellow in Islamic Law at Yale Law School. Abroad, she has served as the Whittlesey Chair of History and Archaeology at the American University of Beirut and held professorships in Oman and China. Readings and productions of her plays have been produced at Lincoln Center, the Public Theatre, City Center, Trinity Repertory Company, Perishable Theatre, Catalyst Theatre, Brown University, and the New York Fringe Festival. She received her MFA in Literary Arts at Brown University.

Dan Pinkerton lives in Urbandale, Iowa.

Ein Kyi Phyu (also known as Catherine) is a blogger and education enthusiast who likes to explore different opportunities in education. Her most heartfelt pleasure lies in sharing her knowledge and experience. Having an academic background in psychology, she has worked as a psychological content writer for Honest Hour Psychological

Services. With a deep interest in community service, she has volunteered in various organizations since her university days.

Currently, she is trying to step into the world of fictional writing and translation. Her first publication was published at Portside Review through Link the Wor(l)ds Literary Translation workshop under the leadership of saya Ko Ko Thett. While working at Parami University, she published her first solo article "Nothing Major, Sir" in *Reflections*, a collaborative issue between SEAM (Yale University) and SIC (Parami University). She is now working as an English language teacher in Yangon, Myanmar as she strives to publish her first collection of flash fictions.

Su Costa Prevost was born and raised near the Mississippi River in New Orleans. She's published prose and poetry in various literary journals and has exhibited her photography in museums and galleries over the years. After a career of teaching ESL, she now devotes her time to writing her first poetry manuscript, entitled *Dear Joe, Etc.* She lives in both New Orleans and in Mexico where she has two burros and four rescue dogs.

Anderson Roeth is a late-blooming writer and editor from Kentucky. He has worked at comic book shops, call centers, and car washes, and for many years, has worked in higher education. He lives in Louisville, Kentucky, with his wife and cat.

John Surowiecki is the author of fifteen poetry books of various sizes and shapes, most recently *The Place of the Solitaires: Poems from Titles by Wallace Stevens*, published in 2023 by Wolfson Press. This month, Bass Clef Books will put out his chapbook, *Chez Pétrouchka*, giving a voice—nasty and foul—to the puppet in the Stravinsky ballet. Surowiecki is also the recipient of the Poetry Foundation Pegasus Award for his verse-play *My Nose and Me (A TragedyLite or TragiDelight in 33 Scenes)* which was presented by the Foundation at the Chicago Shakespeare Theater as part of the Poetry on Stage series. Other prizes include the Nimrod Pablo Neruda Prize for Poetry, The Washington Prize, The White Pine Press Poetry Prize, a Connecticut Artist Fellowship grant in poetry, and a silver medal in the Sunken Garden Poetry Prize. Also: his *Pie Man* won the 2017 Nilsen Prize for a First Novel. Surowiecki, now retired, was a poetry instructor at Manchester Community College and is co-editor of the Connecticut River Review.

Julie Marie Wade is Professor of English & Creative Writing at Florida International University in Miami, where she teaches poetry, memoir, lyric essay, and hybrid forms to graduate and undergraduate students. She is the author of 16 collections of various genres, most recently *Otherwise: Essays*, selected by Lia Purpura as the winner of the 2022 Autumn House Press Nonfiction Prize. Her forthcoming collections are *The Mary*

Years: A Memoir, selected by Michael Martone as the winner of the 2023 Clay Reynolds Novella Prize, and *Quick Change Artist: Poems*, selected by Octavio Quintanilla as the winner of the 2023 Anhinga Press Prize for Poetry. Wade lives with her spouse Angie Griffin and their two cats in Dania Beach.

Miles Waggener is the author of four books of poetry, most recently *Superstition Freeway*, published by The Word Works. His new poems appear or are forthcoming in *Nomadartx, Sugar House Review, Action-Spectacle*, and *Plume Poetry*. He teaches at the University of Nebraska Omaha, where he directs the writing program.

Luke Wallin's 11th book, *The Night we Called the Owls: Stories and Poems*, was published by Ember Press in 2023. He holds an MFA from Iowa and advanced degrees in Regional Planning and Philosophy. He taught at The School of Visual Arts, University College Dublin, Spalding University's MFA in Creative Writing program, and is Professor Emeritus at The University of Massachusetts Dartmouth. Learn more about his books, music, and painting at lukewallin.com.

Cornerstone Contributor's Note

Emma Catherine Hoff is an eleven-year-old writer and poet from New York City, where she lives with her parents and her cat, Gavroche. She is one of the winners of the 2023 Poetry Society's Foyle Young Poets of the Year Award. Her poems have appeared in the *Rattle Young Poets Anthology*, *The Louisville Review*, *The Poetry Society*, and *Stone Soup Magazine*. Her podcast, *Poetry Soup*, as well as book reviews and essays, appear regularly on the Stone Soup Blog. Her first book, a poetry collection, titled *An Archeology of the Future*, was published in the fall of 2023. It won Stone Soup's 2022 Book Contest.

Laurie Fader

About the Cover Artist

Fables, or cautionary tales, with narrative elements embedded in labyrinthian corridors of color, shape, and form can be found in Laurie Fader's recent work. Macabre humor embodies the forces of our salvation from environmental destruction while dreamy alternative realities engage us in her complex, spirited paintings.

Fader has been awarded two Great Meadows Foundation awards, a Pollock-Krasner Grant, an Adolf and Esther Gottlieb Foundation award, and a Helen Winternitz Award for excellence in painting from the Yale School of Art. She has participated in numerous residencies including the Jentel Foundation, Willapa Bay AIR, Virginia Center for the Creative Arts, the American Academy in Rome, Scuola Grafica di Venezia, The International School of Drawing, Painting and Sculpture in Umbria, Italy, the Alfred & Trafford Klotz Residency in France, and a painting fellowship in Haiti. Her recent exhibitions include Susan Eley Gallery in Hudson, NY, Cody Gallery in Arlington, VA, Radiator Gallery in Long Island City, NY, Carter Burden Gallery, and First St Gallery in Chelsea. She is represented by Cavalier Gallery in New York City.

Fader has held teaching positions at the Yale School of Art, Pratt Institute, MICA, Goucher College, and was Chair and co-founder of The Kentucky College of Art and Design at Spalding University in Louisville, Kentucky, where she currently resides as a full-time practicing artist.